D1758185

GLASGOW FROM THE AIR
75 YEARS OF AERIAL PHOTOGRAPHY

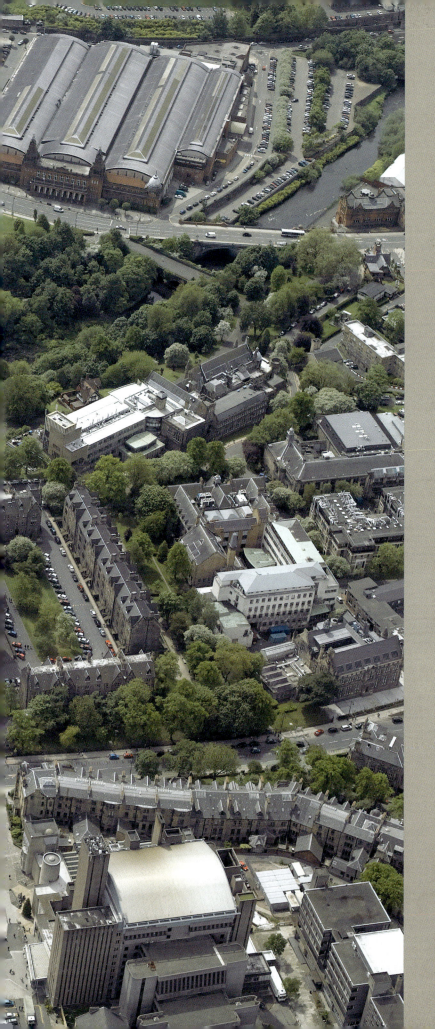

Carol Foreman

GLASGOW
FROM THE AIR

75 YEARS OF AERIAL
PHOTOGRAPHY

BIRLINN LTD IN ASSOCIATION WITH THE
ROYAL COMMISSION ON THE ANCIENT AND
HISTORICAL MONUMENTS OF SCOTLAND

PREVIOUS PAGE.

This excellent view looks south over Glasgow University, Kelvingrove Art Gallery and Museum, and the Kelvin Hall. The circular building in the foreground is the University Reading Room. The tall building to its right is the Library. Separating the University's two quadrangles are the Bute and Randolph Halls. Left in the view is the River Kelvin meandering through Kelvingrove Park and crossing in front of the University before flowing under Partick Bridge, top right in the view. (The bridge with the bus on it). Left of the bridge is the Kelvin Hall, the right hand section housing the Transport Museum. Across Argyle Street from the Kelvin Hall is Kelvingrove Art Gallery and Museum of 1901 that re-opened in 2006 after being closed for three years following a £28 million refurbishment. Glasgow University, Kelvingrove Art Gallery and Museum, and the Kelvin Hall feature in chapter seven – The West End

First published in 2006 by

Birlinn Limited
West Newington House
10 Newington Road
Edinburgh EH9 1QS

www.birlinn.co.uk

In association with the
Royal Commission on the Ancient and
Historical Monuments of Scotland
John Sinclair House
16 Bernard Terrace
Edinburgh EH8 9NX

ISBN 10: 1-84158-474-6
ISBN 13: 978-1-84158-474-4

British Library Cataloguing-in-Publication Data
A catalogue record for this book is available from the British Library

Designed and typeset by Mark Blackadder

Printed and bound in Slovenia
by Associated Agencies Ltd, Oxford

Contents

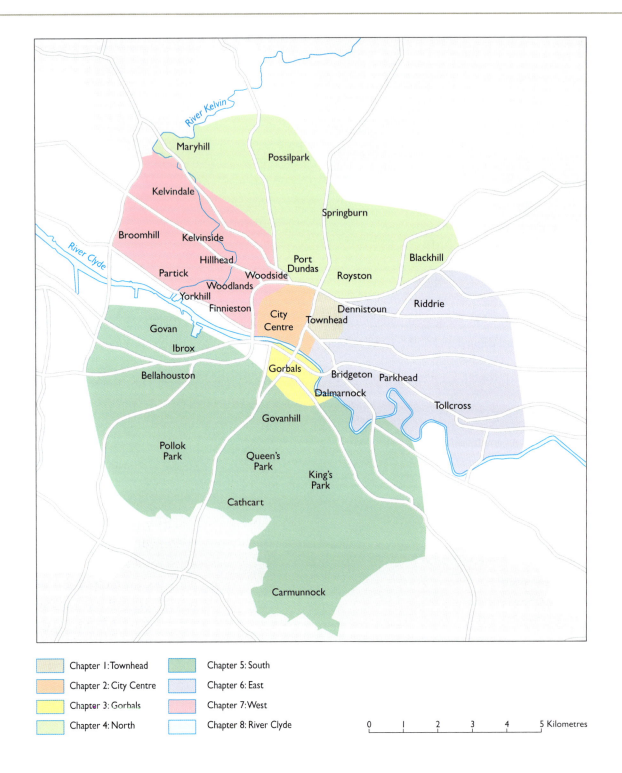

River Kelvin

Maryhill

Possilpark

Kelvindale

Springburn

Broomhill

Kelvinside

River Clyde

Hillhead

Port
Dundas

Blackhill

Partick

Woodside

Royston

Woodlands

Yorkhill

Riddrie

Finnieston

City
Centre

Dennistoun

Townhead

Govan

Ibrox

Gorbals

Bridgeton

Parkhead

Dalmarnock

Bellahouston

Tollcross

Govanhill

Pollok
Park

Queen's
Park

King's
Park

Cathcart

Carmunnock

▦	Chapter 1: Townhead	▦	Chapter 5: South
▦	Chapter 2: City Centre	▦	Chapter 6: East
▦	Chapter 3: Gorbals	▦	Chapter 7: West
▦	Chapter 4: North	▦	Chapter 8: River Clyde

0   1   2   3   4   5 Kilometres

Introduction and Acknowledgements

As aerial views show us that which is not visible from the ground, from them we can discover surprising links between unconnected areas. They also allow us to find large areas of green that we never knew existed, which is especially true of Glasgow with its abundance of parks. Even in built-up areas there is an unexpected greenness. Aerial views also enable us to explore unknown areas for the first time.

The combination of the discovery of the photographic process and the advent of balloon flight in the mid-nineteenth century heralded the development of aerial photography. The application and development of this new technique was accelerated during World War I and from then on the use of the aerial image for military and civilian purposes became commonplace. The German Luftwaffe made an aerial survey of potential targets in Glasgow just before the outbreak of World War II, and the Royal Air Force photographed assets and installations during the war years to check the effectiveness of camouflage schemes. The RAF made regular aerial surveys of the city during the following 20 years and in more recent times commercial survey firms were contracted by the local authority to provide photographs to assist in the planning process. Since 1976, the Royal Commission on the Ancient and Historical Monuments of Scotland (RCAHMS) has contributed to this body of evidence by regularly overflying the city to record photographically the ever-changing townscapes below.

Glasgow from the Air, 75 years of Aerial Photography covers the period from 1930 to 2005 in a series of black and white and colour aerial views of almost every part of the city. Supporting the views is descriptive text with ground photographs illustrating key points. A small vignette with numbered references has been included to help readers identify points of interest. I have used the street and company names applicable at the time the views were taken. As some of the views overlap, inevitably some elements pop up more

than once. Where that has happened, I have tried not to repeat information but to complement it.

To make it easier to identify the districts covered in the book, I have arranged them geographically. For example, the north side of city starts from the west and works eastwards. The south side starts from the east and works westwards.

While the subject of the book is aerial photography, as I have given a brief account of each district before describing its view, it can also serve as a history of the city.

As the book covers 75 years, I have been able to show some before-and-after views that reveal what has and what has not changed during the decades. Surprisingly, while some parts of the city have changed little, others such as Townhead, Cowcaddens, Finnie-ston and Anderston have been completely demolished to make way for the Kingston Bridge, the M8 motorway and the Clyde Expressway, making it almost impossible to recognise the views as being of the same area. From the older views it is apparent just how congested many of the areas were and how closely people lived together.

The majority of aerial photographs in the book come from the national collection of aerial photography of Scotland held in Edinburgh by RCAHMS. The collection can be consulted by appointment. The RCAHMS photographs are Crown copyright. Some views are Air Force Reconnaissance shots taken during the World War II. Others were taken by the Air Force during the 1960s. These are Ministry of Defence copyright. A few views come from the Mitchell Library in Glasgow and Simmons Aerofilms. All photographs are credited except those from my own collection and some loaned by friends.

As the RCAHMS's collection of aerial photographs numbers over one million images ranging from 1940 to 2000, to select those I wanted to use in the book was a mammoth task. After making my selection, however, I realised that I had about four times the number required, so I had to start reducing the pile which took a great deal of time, as those I had chosen were all excellent, making it difficult to discard any. The current views were provided by the RCAHMS's own flying programme, photographer Robert Adam being very willing to find the shots I wanted.

The book is divided into eight chapters each of which opens with a double spread and a list of the districts included.

Chapter 1 covers TOWNHEAD, the district in which Glasgow began and where its thirteenth-century Cathedral is situated along with the oldest house in the city, Provand's Lordship built in 1471.

After Townhead comes the CITY CENTRE, which includes the historic Glasgow Cross (once the heart of the city), the Merchant City and the Commercial Centre.

The next chapter is on THE GORBALS stretching from Kingston to Oatlands. The photographs show the changes that the area has gone through over the decades – from overcrowded tenements cheek-by-jowl with industry to pleasant low-level housing surrounded by green areas.

After the Gorbals come the NORTH, SOUTH, EAST AND WEST districts of the city.

The chapter headed NORTH includes Ruchill, Maryhill, Firhill Park (the home of Partick Thistle), the Forth & Clyde Canal, Possilpark, Port Dundas, Royston, Blochairn, Springburn and Balornock. This chapter shows just how industrial the district once was.

SOUTH begins with a double spread shot of the Burrell Museum after which is a wartime view of the south east covering the Gorbals, Polmadie and Govanhill. The chapter then moves on to Hampden Park, King's Park, Carmunnock, Cathcart, Queen's Park, Langside, Pollok House, Bellahouston Park, Rangers Football Stadium, Ibrox Park and Govan. Although not in Glasgow, the airport has been included. After all, it is called Glasgow International Airport.

The chapter headed EAST is fronted with Tollcross Park. After that is St Andrew's Square then Glasgow Green, the city's oldest park. From the Green it progresses to Bridgeton, Dalmarnock, Parkhead, featuring Celtic Park, Dennistoun and Alexandra Park.

The WEST END chapter starts with a double spread of Great Western Road after which is St George's Cross, Kelvingrove Art Gallery & Museum, the Kelvin Hall, Kelvingrove Park, Park Circus, Glasgow University, the Botanic Gardens and Hillhead.

The last chapter, THE RIVER CLYDE, begins with a shot of the Broomielaw. It then goes downriver from Custom House Quay, the start of Glasgow Harbour and ends at the Rothesay Dock. The older photographs show the docks of the past and the famous shipyards now gone such as Harland & Wolff, Fairfield, Alexander Stephen, Barclay Curle, and the great John Brown yard that built the world acclaimed liners, the *Queen Mary*, the *Queen Elizabeth* and the *QE2*. Strictly speaking, John Brown's yard should not really have been included as it is in Clydebank, but no history of the river would be complete without mention of possibly the greatest shipyard of them all.

There are numerous people I have to thank for their help in getting this book published. To begin with, it could not have been possible without the help of the following people from the RCAHMS: David Easton and Dave Cowley for their knowledge and patience, photographer Robert Adam for his magnificent photography and willingness to make sure I got the views I wanted, and his colleagues in the photographic section for scanning the images. Last, but certainly not least, I thank Kristina Watson who had the hard work of collating the material I had selected.

As well as friends such as Fergus Maitland, whose expertise I always avail myself of, I also have to thank the following for providing information and images: Clydeport, Partick Thistle Football Club, Rangers

Football Club, the Scottish Football Museum, British Waterways Scotland, Caledonian University, the Royal College, Glasgow International Airport, BAe Systems, King's Park Library, Castlemilk Library and especially the Mitchell Library for permission to reproduce views from its Special Collections and from Virtual Mitchell. Special mention as usual goes to Iain Paterson of Glasgow Development & Regeneration Services.

I also thank Clare Crawford for her high standard of editing, Neville Moir of Birlinn, for overseeing production and keeping calm when things were fraught, and designer Mark Blackadder for his creativity in slotting the images and text together. Finally, I thank Hugh Andrew of Birlinn for his encouragement and great support for my writing over a number of years.

CAROL FOREMAN
2006

1

Townhead

Townhead Interchange

Glasgow Cathedral 1998

The Necropolis 1998

Townhead 1950

Strathclyde University
and Townhead Housing Estate 1998

Bell o' the Brae 1930

Townhead Interchange

This view of 2006 shows the loops, twists and turns of the Townhead Interchange (of the M8 motorway, begun in the 1960s) that destroyed old Townhead, leaving the district virtually unrecognisable from that of yesteryear. The right-hand part of the view shows Townhead split in half by the motorway the foundations of which were built over the Monkland Canal and the cut of the junction linking the Monkland and Forth & Clyde Canals. Top right is the modern part of the Royal Infirmary and bottom right, barely in the view, is St Mungo's RC Church (1886) which, along with Charles Rennie Mackintosh's Martyrs' School (1895) nearby but not in the view, is now stranded above the main road instead of being sandwiched amongst tenements as it was previously.

Left of the Royal Infirmary is the district of Royston, once known as Garngad.

Crown copyright RCAHMS Ref. DP9909

1. Glasgow Cathedral
2. Blacader Aisle
3. Old Burial Ground
4. St Mungo Museum of
   Religious Life and Art
5. Royal Infirmary
6. New Burial Ground
7. Necropolis
8. Bridge of Sighs

Glasgow Cathedral 1998

Glasgow Cathedral in the middle of the view is almost dwarfed by the massive bulk of the Royal Infirmary, the second on the site. The first, built on the site of the Bishop's Castle and designed in 1792 by Robert and John Adam, was replaced by a 1901 design by James Miller. It was in an extension to the first building that Joseph Lister began his pioneering work on the principle of antiseptic surgery. He discovered that the use of carbolic acid kept wounds free of germs, allowing operations to be performed more safely.

Left of the Infirmary is the St Mungo Museum of Religious Life and Art, built in Scots Baronial style 1989–92. The museum is divided into three galleries – an Art Gallery, a Religious Life Gallery, and a Gallery of Religion in the West of Scotland.

Until its return to the Art Galleries, in 2006, on view in the museum was Scotland's favourite painting, *Christ of St John of the Cross*, painted by the Spanish surrealist artist Salvador Dali in 1951. Dali's inspiration for the painting was a sketch attributed to the Carmelite friar St John of the Cross (1542–91) after he had a vision of Christ on the cross. Represented in the museum, which also serves as a visitor centre for the Cathedral, are various religious beliefs such as Christianity, Buddhism, Hinduism, Islam, Judaism and Sikhism. Behind the museum is one of Britain's first Japanese Zen gardens.

The Cathedral has the old burial ground on its left and the new burial ground on its right. The Necropolis is in front of it. The single-storey extension in the centre of the Cathedral (south transept) is the Blacader aisle. Recognisable from miles around by its green roof (aged copper), the Cathedral is the most distinguished building in Glasgow and the finest example of pre-Reformation Gothic architecture in Scotland.

Although Glasgow's first proper cathedral was consecrated in 1136, its origin is said to lie in the fourth century, as the area had been sacred since 397. St Ninian, a Briton of noble birth who had been educated in Rome, consecrated a Christian burial place on a piece of ground on the hill slope between the Molendinar stream and a fort built where the Royal Infirmary now is. Glasgow was then called Cathures, the *cathair*, or fort, which, before the Romans came, being a stronghold of the Britons of Strathclyde.

Nothing further is heard of Cathures until 543 when Glasgow's patron saint, St Kentigern, popularly called Mungo, arrived here. According to legend, Mungo was born in 518 near Culross where St Serf raised and trained him for the priesthood. When

The Adam brothers' Royal Infirmary. Although the decision to demolish the historic building caused great controversy, as was usual in Glasgow, this was ignored and it was taken down in 1912, losing Glasgow yet another Adam building. In 1924, despite pleas, the Infirmary managers decided that the Lister Ward in the surgical block in an extension added to the hospital in 1861 should be pulled down. Fortunately, there is a reconstruction of the ward in the Wellcome Medical Museum in London and the Royal Faculty of Physicians and Surgeons in Glasgow was gifted the fireplace from the ward and a table.

Mungo left St Serf he came to Carnock (near what is now Stirling) where he found a holy man, Fergus, on his deathbed. Fergus's dying wish was that his body should be placed on a cart drawn by two untamed oxen and that Mungo was to follow the oxen and, where they stopped, he was to bury Fergus. The oxen stopped at St Ninian's burial ground, and the place where Fergus was buried is now marked by an inscription in the vault of the Blacader, or Fergus, aisle in the Cathedral, that reads 'This is ye ile of Car Fergus'.

Mungo settled beside the burial ground and founded a religious community. His little Church of the Holy Trinity became, in the Middle Ages, the Cathedral of St Mungo. When he was twenty-five, the king, clergy and the people chose him to be their bishop. The history of St Kentigern tells us that on his election as bishop he established his cathedral seat in a town called Glasgu. When the name came into being is not indicated. Some years after he settled in Glasgu, persecution by the apostate King Morken compelled Mungo to flee to Wales where he founded a monastic community, St Asaph's.

After the battle of Arthuret in 573, the new king of Strathclyde, the Christian Rhydderch Hael, invited Mungo to return to Glasgu where he was welcomed. St Columba visited Mungo in Glasgu, and on the banks of the Molendinar they exchanged their pastoral staves 'in token of the esteem they bore for each other'. (Two windows in the Cathedral's upper chapterhouse depict St Mungo and St Columba meeting and St Mungo baptising converts.) When Mungo died in 603, he was buried in his church, which, with the adjoining dwellings of wood and wattles, was the origin of the city of Glasgow.

After the death of St Mungo, a curtain falls on the story of Glasgow for five centuries. Nothing is known

Left. The remaining twelfth-century vaulting shaft from Bishop Jocelin's cathedral. Note the different size and shape of the pillar's capital compared to that on the pillar to the right.

Below. Apart from the twelfth-century cathedral vaulting shaft, this photograph shows the only other reminder of the church of that date. It is a *voussoir*, a wedge-shaped stone from an arch, plastered and painted on two sides. It is displayed in the Chapel of St John the Evangelist, and it is one of only two known examples surviving of the art of wall painting in medieval Scotland.

Opposite. St Mungo's tomb in the lower church. It stands in a space formed by four columns directly below the site of the altar above and designed to carry its weight. Under the vaulting a lamp is kept burning.

of the church Mungo founded until the future King David restored the see and Bishop John Achaius began building Glasgow's first proper cathedral, which was consecrated in 1136. When fire destroyed it in 1175, Bishop Jocelin laid the foundations for a new building that was consecrated in 1197. Jocelin's building was never finished, and of it, only a single wall-shaft resting upon a fragment of bench-table remains near the southwest entrance to the lower church.

Bishop William de Bondington (1233–58), began the Cathedral we see today. He completed the quire and lower church. The nave was not completed until the end of the thirteenth century. Bishop Lauder (1408–26) was responsible for rebuilding the splendid central tower and spire after they were damaged by lightning.

Bishop Cameron 'the magnificent' (1426–46) built much of the sacristy and finished the chapterhouse. He also erected the consistory house at the southwest elevation of the Cathedral. Both the consistory house, which in ancient records was known as the library, and the northwest tower, thought to be coeval with the nave, were removed in Victorian times despite a public outcry about the mutilation of the Cathedral. The priceless contents of the library were burned.

The last of the builders, the first archbishop of Glasgow, Robert Blacader (1483–1508), erected the quire screen. Although built around 1250, the single-storey aisle that protrudes from the Cathedral southwards is named after Archbishop Blacader as he covered it with stone vaulting around 1500. It was the last addition to the Cathedral and is said to cover the spot where St Mungo buried the holy man, Fergus. With its white-washed stonework and colourful ceiling bosses, the Blacader aisle is the brightest part of the Cathedral.

The tomb of St Mungo is in the Lower Church, often wrongly called the Crypt since it is not below ground. Thousands of pilgrims came to Glasgow in medieval times to worship at the tomb and at a silver shrine behind the high altar where the saint's remains

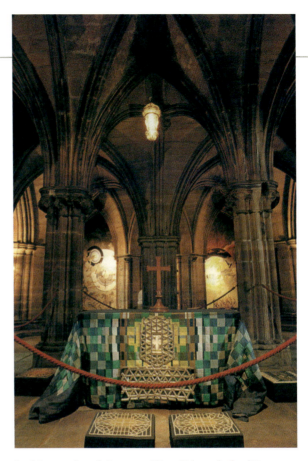

had been placed. In 1301, King Edward, the 'Hammer of the Scots', was among the pilgrims. In 1451, the Pope decreed that a pilgrimage to Glasgow Cathedral would be as meritorious as to make one to Rome.

Glasgow Cathedral suffered during the stormy days of the Reformation. Archbishop Beaton fled to France in 1560, taking with him most of the relics, jewels and ornaments. Fortunately, the men of the various trades were able to persuade the townspeople to spare the structure when they marched on the Cathedral in their zeal to cleanse all churches of popery It was the only cathedral on mainland Scotland to escape destruction at the hands of the reformers. While the fabric was saved, the altars, vestments and images were destroyed, together with a valuable library. After the Reformation, the Cathedral was divided into three to serve three congregations: the Outer High, the Inner High, and the Barony.

Today, the Church of Scotland worships in the Cathedral, which is Crown property maintained by Historic Scotland. Visitors are welcome.

The Necropolis 1998

The Necropolis, to the east of Glasgow Cathedral, is the city's most spectacular graveyard, not only because of its magnificent monuments but also because of its hillside position from which there are outstanding views over the city. This photograph provides an excellent view of the cemetery, which is divided into sections named after letters from the Greek alphabet such as Alpha, Beta, Delta, Omega, Epsilon and Lambda. In addition, there are six sections with Latin numerals – Primus, Secundus, Tertius, Quartus, Quintus and Sextus.

Modelled on the famous Père Lachaise cemetery in Paris, the Necropolis was Scotland's first 'hygienic' graveyard and described as the 'parent of all the garden cemeteries throughout Scotland'. Built on the Fir Park, a recreation ground owned by the Merchants' House, it was carefully planned to prevent the spread of infectious diseases such as cholera and typhoid. It was also special in that it was non-denominational.

There were two burials before the Necropolis's official opening on 12 March 1833. The first was that of a Jew, Joseph Levy, who died of cholera in September 1832, the second that of Elizabeth Miles, the superintendent's stepmother, who was buried in February 1833. A special enclosure for Jewish burials was opened in 1836 but by 1857, it had closed because there was no more space available as Jews are buried with strictly one body to each grave.

The entrance to the Necropolis is from Cathedral Square, but before entering the graveyard, the Bridge of Sighs, middle right in the picture, has to be crossed. Built in 1833 to span the ravine through which the Molendinar Burn once flowed, the bridge received its name because of the many funeral processions crossing over it.

The graveyard contains tombs and monuments of prominent nineteenth-century Glaswegians, and as many of them had their memorials designed in the style of the place where they made their money, almost every kind of architecture in the world is represented, much of it the work of Glasgow's leading architects. On the right in the view, its design inspired by the Church of the Holy Sepulchre in Jerusalem, is the grandest mausoleum (1855), that of Major Archibald Douglas Monteath, an officer who served in the East India Company.

Glasgow's oldest commercial business, Tennent's Wellpark Brewery said to have been founded in 1556, is in the top right-hand corner of the view. There is a large memorial to the Tennents of Wellpark in the Necropolis. The Cathedral and the Royal Infirmary are at the bottom of this view.

This photograph shows some of the elaborate memorials in the Necropolis. The largest is that of John Henry Alexander, an actor and proprietor of the Theatre Royal in Dunlop Street. On the Italianate monument are items and words emblematic of the theatre as well as the words: 'All the world's a stage, And all the Men and Women merely Players'. Left of Alexander's monument, at the highest point of the graveyard, is a Doric column crowned by a statue of John Knox erected by public subscription in 1825 in what was then Fir Park. On the base are the words: 'The chief instrument, under God of the Reformation in Scotland'. Beside Knox is the tomb of Duncan Macfarlan DD, a Principal of Glasgow University when it was in the High Street. He also became minister of Glasgow Cathedral in 1824. The circular canopied monument near Macfarlan's tomb belongs to the Rev. John Dick, minister of Greyfriars Church, which stood in Albion Street. The site of that church is now a car park.
Crown copyright RCAHMS Ref. B17917CN

1. Royal Infirmary
2. The Cathedral
3. Bridge of Sighs
4. The Monteath Mausoleum
5. Tennent's Wellpark Brewery
6. John Knox's Statue
7. The Necropolis

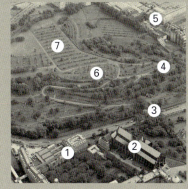

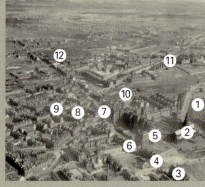

1. Necropolis
2. The Cathedral
3. Barony Church
4. Provand's Lordship
5. Royal Infirmary
6. Barony Free Church
7. Castle Street
8. Martyrs' School
9. St Mungo's RC Church
10. Monkland Canal
11. Townhead and Blochairn Church
12. St Rollox railway works

Townhead 1950

This congested view of Townhead was taken before the area was largely demolished to make way for the Townhead Interchange. Castle Street runs diagonally across the photograph. The Cathedral is bottom right with the Necropolis to its right and the Royal Infirmary to its left. Directly left of the Infirmary is the Barony Free Church the 120-foot tower of which was a landmark. In 1973, the church was demolished following damage caused by the nearby Post Office tunnel.

In front of the Infirmary is Provand's Lordship, Glasgow's oldest house, the only medieval building near the Cathedral to have survived the nineteenth-century clearances. Built in 1471, it was the manse for the adjoining St Nicholas Hospital and later the town house for the Canon of Barlanark, or Provan. It got its name because the Canon's rectory was known as the Lordship of Provan.

Mary Queen of Scots stayed in Provand's Lordship when she came to Glasgow in 1566 to visit her sick husband, Lord Darnley, and it is said that the 'Casket Letters', which were supposed to implicate her in the murder of Darnley, may have been written while she was there. Queen Elizabeth the late Queen Mother took tea in the house after she had unveiled the Memorial Windows in the Cathedral on 2 September 1954. The house is open to the public. In front of Provand's Lordship is the Gothic-style Barony Church (1886–90) by J. J. Burnet and J. A. Campbell, now a ceremonial and graduation hall for Strathclyde University.

The left-hand quarter of the picture shows a densely tenemented area intermingled with industry, schools and churches. It also shows just how closely Glaswegians lived to each other. In the nineteenth century, the social conditions in this part of the city were appalling, its tenements being a breeding ground for disease.

Among the tenements in Parson Street is Charles Rennie Mackintosh's Martyrs' School (1895), named after Covenanters James Lawson, James Nisbet and Alexander Wood who were executed on the spot (once Howgate Prison) in 1684. As Mackintosh's work was so highly thought of, when the school was threatened with demolition, protests to save it came from as far away as the Louvre Museum in Paris. (Mackintosh was born in Parson Street.) West of Martyrs' School is St Mungo's RC Church, one of the oldest Catholic churches in Glasgow, the foundation stone being laid in 1866.

From the centre of the view to the right is the Monkland Canal, now replaced by the M8 motorway. Above the canal is Royston, or Garngad as it was previously known and to the left are the St Rollox railway works. Townhead and Blochairn Parish Church sits on Garngad Hill.

This 2005 photograph of the same area as that opposite shows how dramatically it has changed. The Townhead Interchange dominates the scene. The densely tenemented area has vanished, leaving the Martyrs' School and St Mungo's Church stranded above the main road. The Royal Infirmary now stretches as far as the motorway and round into Alexandra Parade. The canal has gone, the motorway having been constructed over it. There is new housing at Royston, and all that remains of Townhead and Blochairn Parish Church is its landmark steeple. Provand's Lordship now stands on its own, its adjoining tenements having been demolished. Opposite Provand's Lordship is the St Mungo Museum of Religion and Art, built between 1989 and 1992 in a style intended to echo that of the Bishop's Castle, on whose site it is set.

Today Townhead, west of the Cathedral, bears no resemblance to the Townhead of yesteryear. In the 1960s, a sweeping redevelopment replaced the dense mixture of tenements and industrial buildings with high- and low-rise blocks of housing and educational buildings that now form Strathclyde University.

This photograph shows Townhead looking east towards the Cathedral. The University campus stretches from George Street to St James Road, with Cathedral Street in the middle. Extreme right in the bottom quarter of the picture is the massive Royal College on George Street, built from 1901 for the Glasgow and West of Scotland Technical College. The 'Tech', as it was known, was a descendant of the Andersonian Institution, founded in 1795. From it grew Glasgow's second university, which received its charter in 1964. Centre right in the picture, in the middle of the university campus, is the Glasgow Royal Maternity Hospital in Rottenrow, a grey, dismal mass of Edwardian buildings and additions, now demolished and the site landscaped.

Near the university's buildings are two striking landmarks – the tall building centre bottom in the view and the one behind it. Both built in 1963, the taller one, the Glasgow College of Building and Printing, has thirteen storeys, and the shorter one, the Central College of Commerce, seven storeys. Left of the College of Commerce is the former St Andrew Free Church, now a furniture store.

In the middle of the picture is Allan Glen's School, founded in 1853 as Glasgow's first school for training in science and practical subjects. It was in the original building at the corner of Cathedral Street and North Hanover Street that Charles Rennie Mackintosh was educated. The present 1960s building is now part of the College of Commerce.

The whole of the left-hand side of the view shows the high- and low-rise housing that replaced the closely packed nineteenth-century tenements shown in the previous view. All that remains are Rennie Mackintosh's Martyrs' School and St Mungo's RC Church, top centre in the view, both alienated above the main road. In front of them is the Townhead Interchange, and to their right, the Royal Infirmary with the Cathedral on its right.

This architectural drawing shows the massive red sandstone Royal College in George Street designed in 1901 by David Barclay. Its origin lies in the Andersonian Institution (originally called 'university') founded through a bequest from John Anderson, Professor of Natural Philosophy (physics) at the University of Glasgow. He wished to make it possible for working-class mechanics to receive an education that would qualify them for an industrial or trade profession. Because Professor Anderson so delighted in explosive demonstrations, his students nicknamed him 'Jolly Jack Phosphorus'.

1. St Andrew Free Church
2. Central College of Commerce
3. Glasgow College of Building and Printing
4. The Royal College
5. Glasgow Royal Maternity Hospital
6. Cathedral Street
7. Allan Glen's School
8. St Mungo's RC Church
9. Martyrs' School
10. The Royal Infirmary
11. Glasgow Cathedral

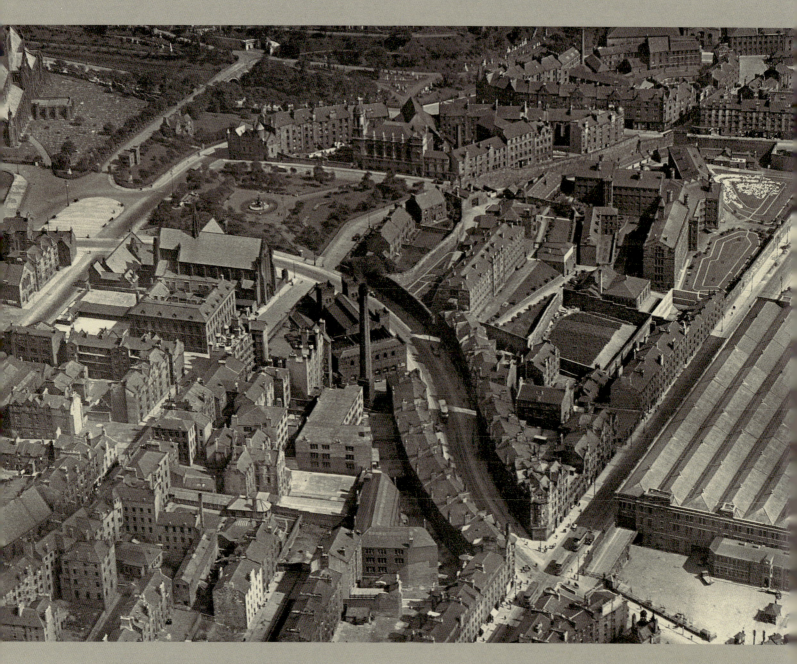

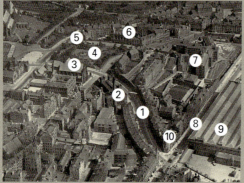

1. Bell o' the Brae (upper High Street)
2. Hydraulic Pumping Station
3. The Barony Church
4. Cathedral Square Gardens
5. Cathedral House
6. Barony North Church
7. Duke Street Prison
8. Duke Street
9. High Street Goods Station
10. City Improvement Trust houses

Bell o' the Brae (upper High Street) 1930

Simmons Aerofilms

The curved street bisecting the view was known as the Bell o' the Brae, a term applied to the highest part of the slope of a hill – bel signifying a prominence. The street runs from High Street down to Duke Street on the right of the picture. It was here that Sir William Wallace, with the help of his uncle, Auchinleck, defeated an English force in 1297. The English were garrisoned in the Bishops' Castle (where the Royal Infirmary now stands). Doubt has been cast on the authenticity of this story, but all histories of Glasgow include it. Red sandstone 1901 Arts and Crafts versions of seventeenth-century Scottish tenements replaced the thatched cottages and eighteenth- and nineteenth-century tenements that once lined the street.

The tall chimney near the top of the street belongs to the building in front of it, a hydraulic pumping station built in 1893 in Scots baronial style with two crenellated towers. It was demolished in 1973. Left of the pumping station is the red sandstone Barony Church (1886–9) the façade of which resembles Dunblane Cathedral. Inside there are many fine stained-glass windows, such as the one portraying the meeting of St Columba and St Mungo.

Facing the Barony Church across Cathedral Square Gardens is the Italianate Barony North Church (1878).

Built for the United Presbyterians and taken over by the Evangelical Assembly in 1978, it is the only church in Glasgow featuring as a group life-sized statues of the apostles Matthew, Mark, Luke and John. These are across the roof edge. Above the main doors are figures representing St Peter and St Paul. Left of the church is the red sandstone baronial-style Cathedral House, built in 1896 for the Discharged Prisoners Aid Society, which during its lifetime helped around 500,000 ex-prisoners.

On the extreme right in the view is the North British Railway's massive High Street Goods Station. Today all that remains is the outer wall along Duke Street. The forbidding group of buildings left of the station belong to Duke Street Prison, the main jail of Glasgow until the opening of Barlinnie Prison in 1882, upon which Duke Street became largely a women's prison. From 1865 to the 1920s, hangings took place in the prison yard. Susan Newell, the last woman to be hanged in Scotland, was executed there in 1923. The prison had a flagpole on which a black flag was hoisted when an execution took place. After an execution a bell (on display at the People's Palace) was tolled. Duke Street Prison was demolished in 1950 and replaced by the Ladywell Housing Scheme.

Seventeenth-century thatched cottages in the Bell o' the Brae, the name given to the steep part of High Street that led to the Cathedral. During the eighteenth and nineteenth centuries, the gradient of the Bell o' the Brae was lowered. While old buildings like this were picturesque, in reality the ramshackle inflammable buildings were vermin-ridden breeding grounds for disease and horrendous to live in.

City Centre

General View of the City Centre

This 2006 view covers central Glasgow. The thoroughfare running diagonally from right to left across the bottom of the view is Buchanan Street, the city's most prestigious shopping area, and parallel to it is Queen Street. In the middle is George Square, with Queen Street Station to its left. The City Chambers occupy the east side of the square. The right-hand side of the view covers the Merchant City, where buildings such as Hutcheson's Hall, the Trades' Hall and the Ramshorn Church are situated. Top left is Townhead with to its right across Cathedral Street, Strathclyde University. The park in the centre of the campus was created out of the site once occupied by Rottenrow Maternity Hospital. *Crown copyright RCAHMS Ref. DP9910*

Glasgow Cross 2006

Originally, Glasgow's Mercat Cross was near the Cathedral at the High Street/Rottenrow/Drygate intersection. When the centre of commerce shifted from the upper town to the lower town after the Reformation, it moved to the High Street/Saltmarket/Gallowgate/Trongate intersection. Glasgow Cross was the hub of the city from the Middle Ages until the eighteenth century. It was where, in 1707, the Articles of Union were burned and where, in December 1745, Bonnie Prince Charlie's Highlanders proclaimed him Regent of Scotland.

This photograph shows Glasgow Cross's two ancient steeples. In the centre is the older, the Tolbooth Steeple (1626), a tall slender, seven-storey square tower with a Gothic crown spire. The steeple, marooned in the middle of High Street, was once attached to the Tolbooth, the city's civic centre and prison outside which hangings took place. A special payment was made in 1698 to the jailer for the extra work involved in keeping 'warlocks and witches' locked up in the Tolbooth. Until 1790, the steeple bore spikes to accommodate the heads of malefactors. The prison featured in Sir Walter Scott's famous work *Rob Roy*. Twice in its lifetime, the steeple has been threatened with destruction, first in 1814 and again in 1922.

Middle left in the view is the second of the Cross's steeples, the Gothic Tron (1636), once part of the Tron-St Mary's Church, accidentally burned down by drunken members of the Hell Fire Club on Valentine's Day in 1793. The steeple was untouched. Pedestrian arches were cut through it in 1855. The replacement church (1793) is now the Tron Theatre. The word 'tron' derives from the public tron, or weighing machine, once situated at the Mercat Cross.

The building opposite the Tron Steeple, a turreted Baronial extravaganza designed by J. T. Rochead for the ill-fated City of Glasgow Bank (1855), was intended to complement the ancient buildings then surviving in the area.

Right of the Tolbooth Steeple is the octagonal Mercat Cross. It is not the original but a 1930 replica of a seventeenth-century Scottish mercat cross with a proclamation platform and unicorn-topped column. The architect was Edith Burnet Hughes, the only woman to have designed one of Glasgow's listed buildings. The original Cross was removed in 1659. Right of the Cross, dwarfing it, is Mercat Buildings (1925).

The long range of buildings top right in the view are former railway warehouses built in Bell Street in 1882–3 for the Glasgow & South Western railway and now converted into housing and offices.

The City of Glasgow Union Railway running diagonally across the picture marks the boundary between the city centre and the east end. The junction at Glasgow Cross now has five offshoots, London Road having been added to the original four.

Crown copyright RCAHMS Ref DP9918

Glasgow Cross in 1977. The Tolbooth Steeple stands like a stone policeman in the middle of High Street. The Tolbooth, St Giles in Edinburgh and King's College Aberdeen are the only three ancient buildings remaining in Scotland with a crown spire. The views from the top of the Tolbooth are stunning – to the north the Cathedral, to the west Trongate, to the south Saltmarket, and to the east Gallowgate. To the disappointment of many, the public are not allowed into the steeple.

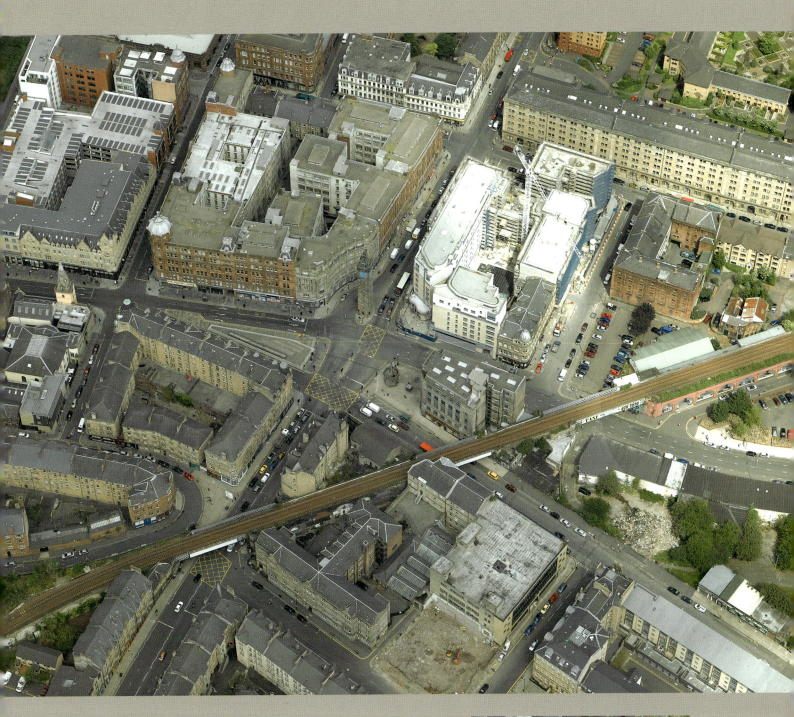

1. Tolbooth Steeple
2. High Street
3. Bell Street Warehouses
4. Gallowgate
5. London Road
6. City of Glasgow Union Railway
7. Mercat Buildings
8. Mercat Cross
9. Saltmarket
10. Trongate
11. Tron Steeple
12. City of Glasgow Bank

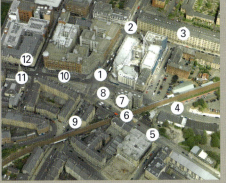

1. Glasgow Green
2. Saltmarket
3. City Mortuary
4. High Court of Justiciary
5. Albert Bridge
6. City of Glasgow Union
   Railway viaduct
7. Former Fish Market
   and Merchant's Steeple
8. St Andrew-by-the-Green
   Church

Saltmarket 2006

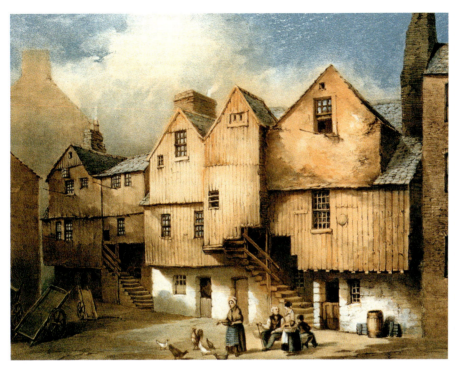

This view from Thomas Fairbairn's *Relics of Ancient Architecture and Other Picturesque Scenes in Glasgow*, published in 1885, shows wooden seventeenth-century houses in a close at 77 Saltmarket. Houses of this kind were erected for the cheapness of materials and for economy of building space. To accomplish the latter purpose, beams were projected from the first storey and an out-shot additional structure raised on them. Such houses once formed the majority of the closes in Saltmarket, but after a great fire of 1677 when the upper part of the street on both sides was destroyed along with tenements in the Gallowgate, few timber houses were erected. Those in the photograph were pulled down by the City Improvement Trust.
Crown copyright RCAHMS Ref. A75028CN

Saltmarket, the straight street running diagonally across the photograph, continues the line of High Street to the river. Saltmarket was once the site of a market selling salt for curing salmon and herring, hence the name. Previously it was Waulkergate, 'the way to the colony of fullers or cloth waulkers', who lived in a cluster of houses near the river. Saltmarket was once a prestigious address. Oliver Cromwell stayed here, as did James VII when he was Duke of York. From the 1870s, the City Improvement Trust, a body concerned with the removal of the central slums, began building the tenements now lining the street, their gables and crowsteps acknowledging the original seventeenth-century dwellings.

Saltmarket ends at Albert Bridge (1871), extreme left in the view. The building beside the bridge is the Greek Revival-style High Court designed by William Stark in 1809. Originally, it housed the municipal offices, the justiciary courts and a jail. The last public hanging in Glasgow took place in front of the jail. It was that of Dr Pritchard who poisoned his wife and mother-in-law. Pritchard was known as the 'Human Crocodile' as he had his wife's coffin lid opened so that he could kiss his victim on the lips. In 1865, 30,000 people watched him hang. The last large gathering of people at the court's main entrance was in 1956. They were awaiting news of the trial of mass murderer Peter Manual.

Right of the High Court is the City Mortuary. The ground it was built on was where people who had been hanged in public were buried, and, apparently while digging the mortuary's foundations workmen came across the skeleton of Dr Pritchard.

Right of the court is Glasgow Green where the Glasgow Fair was once held. From the foot of Saltmarket down to the river there would be circuses, merry-go-rounds, freak shows, booths and beer tents. The Fair is still held on the Green, but at the eastern end.

A railway viaduct leading to the City Union Railway Bridge curves across the view. Left of the bridge is the former fish market (1872) in Bridgegate which envelops the Merchants' Steeple (1669), once the centrepiece of the Merchants' House built on the site in 1659.

Glasgow Cross to George Square 1950

The former Fish Market that envelops the seventeenth-century Merchants' Steeple, the only remaining part of the Merchants' Hall where all the great assemblies and balls were held as, at the time, Bridgegate was the city's most fashionable area.
Crown copyright RCAHMS Ref. B32500

This busy photograph looks north over the city from Clyde Street. East to west, it covers the area between Glasgow Cross and George Square. The sweep of railway tracks leading to St Enoch Station stands out clearly. Extreme middle right is the Tolbooth Steeple of 1626 at Glasgow Cross. North of the steeple are the College and High Street Goods Stations. College Goods Station was built on the ground once occupied by the Old College, which moved to Gilmorehill in 1870. When the College was destroyed, the city lost some of Scotland's most remarkable seventeenth-century architecture. Beyond the Goods Stations are the Royal Infirmary, the Cathedral and the Necropolis.

Left in the view, slightly up from extreme middle, is the City Chambers, right of which, in Ingram Street, is Hutchesons' Hall with, to its right, the Ramshorn Church and graveyard, all of which feature in subsequent views.

To the right in the foreground is the fish market in Bridgegate, begun in 1872 and extended in 1886 and 1903. Incorporated into the building is the Merchants' Steeple, once the focal point of the Merchants' Hall that, along with its hospital, was built on the site in 1659. When the hall was demolished in 1817 to make way for tenement building, the steeple was left standing, and in 1821 the merchants gave it to the city 'on condition of the Town keeping up the Steeple and Clock in all time coming'. After the fish market moved to Blochairn in 1977, the market was unsuccessfully converted into a shopping centre in the fashion of London's Covent Garden. It is now awaiting a new use.

In the foreground to the left is St Andrew's RC Cathedral, opened in 1816 as a chapel for Glasgow's growing Irish Catholic population. The church became a cathedral in 1889. Designed by James Gillespie Graham, it was the first neo-Gothic church in Glasgow. A matching college was planned but was never built for financial reasons.

With its tall octagonal buttresses panelled with tracery rising into turrets on either side of the street gable and a gabled niche containing a statue of St Andrew at its apex, St Andrew's RC Cathedral is an elegant building. It cost £16,000 and during its construction an incensed mob, reminiscent of the Reformation rabble, desecrated it. To put an end to the vandalism, night patrols were organised. In contrast to the intolerance of the mob, the Protestant community contributed over £400 to the building fund. *Courtesy of Glasgow Development and Regeneration Services*

1. St Andrew's RC Cathedral
2. St Enoch Station
3. The City Chambers
4. Hutchesons' Hall
5. Ramshorn Church
6. Royal Infirmary
7. Cathedral
8. Necropolis
9. High Street Goods Station
10. College Goods Station
11. Tolbooth Steeple
12. Fish Market and Merchants' Steeple

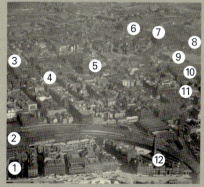

1. Central Station
2. Argyle Street
3. St Enoch Hotel
4. St Enoch Station
5. Lewis's Department Store
6. College Goods Station
7. High Street Goods Station

St Enoch Station and Hotel and Central Station 1953

Simmons Aerofilms

This view of the city taken from the west shows two of Glasgow's passenger railway stations. In the middle of the right-hand half of the view are St Enoch Station and St Enoch Hotel, built for the Glasgow and South Western Railway in 1873. A case of bad judgement by Glasgow's Planning Department in the 1970s was the demolition of the stunning Gothic style St Enoch Hotel. Regarded as the 'most imposing structure in Glasgow' when it opened in 1879, the hotel was the largest in Scotland. The hotel's 1906 price list included rooms at four shillings a night, breakfast or luncheon three shillings and dinner five shillings. Despite an outcry and final attempts to save the well-known landmark, it was demolished in 1977 and replaced by the giant glass St Enoch Shopping Centre.

Behind the hotel is the station's magnificent arched train shed, the first public area in Glasgow to be lit by electricity. The station opened in 1876 and by 1880 was Scotland's premier passenger terminal. When Queen Victoria came to Glasgow in August 1888 to visit the International Exhibition in Kelvingrove Park, it was into St Enoch Station that her train steamed. Express trains ran to Ayrshire and to Stranraer, providing a connection with the Irish steamers.

There was also a coastal service to Greenock where steamers plied to Dunoon, Rothesay and the Kyles of Bute, all popular holiday destinations for Glaswegians. Central Station eventually outclassed St Enoch Station, and it closed in 1966.

Argyle Street bisects the view vertically. In the centre of it, left of the St Enoch train shed, is what was Glasgow's favourite department store, Lewis's (1932), now occupied by Debenhams.

In the foreground is Central Station, built for the Caledonian Railway in 1879. Fronting Gordon Street and Hope Street, it was built on the site of Grahamston, the village that lay between Union Street and Hope Street. In the early 1900s on Fair Saturday, the station heaved with holidaymakers waiting for the boat trains to start them off on their way to Gourock, Wemyss Bay and Ardrossan. The station once had the largest signal box in the world. A feature of the station was its train indicator, which had a panel for each of its thirteen platforms. It was so large that it was visible from every part of the concourse. Now the indicator is electronic.

Top left are more railway buildings, the massive College and High Street Goods Stations, both demolished.

ST. ENOCH STATION. GLASGOW.

This photograph shows the magnificent St Enoch Hotel around the beginning of the twentieth century. When it opened, it had 200 bedrooms, 20 public rooms and a staff of 80. The main frontage on the east of St Enoch Square had a terraced carriageway with a central iron and glass veranda. Also in the picture is the St Enoch Subway Station (1896), a pretty, diminutive castle-like building by James Miller and now the Travel Centre.

St Enoch Centre 2005

Dominating this view is the massive bulk of the St Enoch Centre, which replaced the St Enoch Hotel and Station. When it opened in 1989, it was the largest glass-covered shopping mall in Europe, giving rise to Glaswegians naming it 'Europe's largest greenhouse'. The large building behind the Centre is Debenham's department store, once Lewis's, Scotland's largest department store.

Left of the centre is St Enoch Square, planned in 1768 as a select residential area and laid out around an existing church of the same name. Until its demolition in 1925, a replacement church of 1827 by David Hamilton that retained the original steeple closed the vista down Buchanan Street. St Enoch is a corruption of St Thenaw, the name of the mother of St Mungo, and the area got its name from the ancient chapel dedicated to St Thenaw once there.

In the square is the delightful Jacobean-style Travel Centre designed in 1896 by the foremost railway architect of the time, James Miller, as the St Enoch Subway Station ticket-office. The subway was constructed between 1890 and 1896. Leading north from the square is Buchanan Street, often described as Glasgow's 'Regent Street', which terminates to the north with the Buchanan Galleries shopping centre and the Royal Concert Hall.

In the foreground to the right, in Clyde Street, is St Andrew's RC Cathedral, previously covered. The second last building to the left in Clyde Street is the Greek Doric-style former Custom House (1840) designed by John Taylor, the Irish-born customs official also responsible for Dundee Customs House.

Crown copyright RCAHMS Ref. DP9900

The Merchant City 2005

Crown copyright RCAHMS Ref. DP9899

This view shows most of the Merchant City, which lies at the heart of Glasgow's city centre. It stretches from High Street to Queen Street and from Argyle Street to George Street.

The area is rich in historic buildings, starting bottom right with the Ramshorn Church (proper name St David's) in Ingram Street (1824), the work of Birmingham architect Thomas Rickman. It is among Scotland's first examples of Gothic Revival style, and Rickman decorated its square front tower with pinnacles. The church, now used as a theatre by Strathclyde University, has a fine collection of stained-glass windows. The pavement outside the church was once part of the graveyard of the previous church, and the paving stones with the initials R.F. and A.F. cover the grave of the Foulis brothers who founded the first School of Art.

As the graveyard predates the church, it contains tombstones of Glasgow's famous tobacco lords, such as John Glassford, after whom Glassford Street is named. Pierre Emile L'Angelier, allegedly poisoned by his lover, Madeleine Smith, lies in a grave marked Fleming. Madeleine's trial in 1857 is one of Scotland's most famous. Although she was probably guilty, the verdict was 'not proven'. Some of the graves have iron grilles bolted over them to prevent grave robbing.

West of the church is Hutchesons' Hall, designed by David Hamilton in 1802 and owned by the National Trust for Scotland. It was originally offices and a meeting hall for Hutchesons' Trust, which provided pensions for the needy, and a charity school. The name commemorates brothers George and Thomas Hutcheson who, in the seventeenth century, founded a hospital in Trongate for 'aged and decrepit men of the age above fifty years'. Flanking the principal storey of Hutchesons' Hall are statues of the brothers taken from the seventeenth-century hospital.

Opposite Hutchesons' Hall is the former Sheriff Court (1844), which fills a whole block of the Merchant City. Once it incorporated the county offices, sheriff court and the Merchants' House. West of the court is the Trades' House (1791–4), Glasgow's only surviving Adam building and its oldest secular building in the city still used for its original purpose. Other Adam buildings were the original Royal Infirmary and the Old College Library.

Top left, in Royal Exchange Place, is the Gallery of Modern Art, which started life in 1780 as the country mansion of the tobacco lord William Cunningham. In 1827, with the addition of a portico and a newsroom at the back designed by David Hamilton, it became the Royal Exchange. It is easy to identify the mansion house in the centre of the building.

Near the centre of the view are the City Chambers and George Square, which feature in the following view.

The Palladian-style Trades' House designed by Robert Adam and built between 1791 and 1794. It was originally established as a meeting place for the city's fourteen incorporated trades: hammermen, tailors, cordiners, maltmen, weavers, bakers, skinners, wrights, coopers, fleshers, masons, gardeners, barbers, and bonnetmakers and dyers. Although the origin of many of the guilds is ancient, they were not incorporated until 1605. While the building has been altered or added to, the façade is typically Adam, with a central feature based on a Greek temple design framed by twin Ionic columns. Above the façade is a belfry with a bell that is rung on special occasions such as the Deacon's choosing day.

1. Ramshorn Church
2. Hutchesons' Hall
3. Former Sheriff Court
4. Trades' House
5. Gallery of Modern Art
6. George Square
7. City Chambers

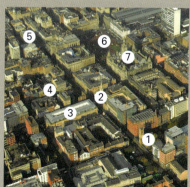

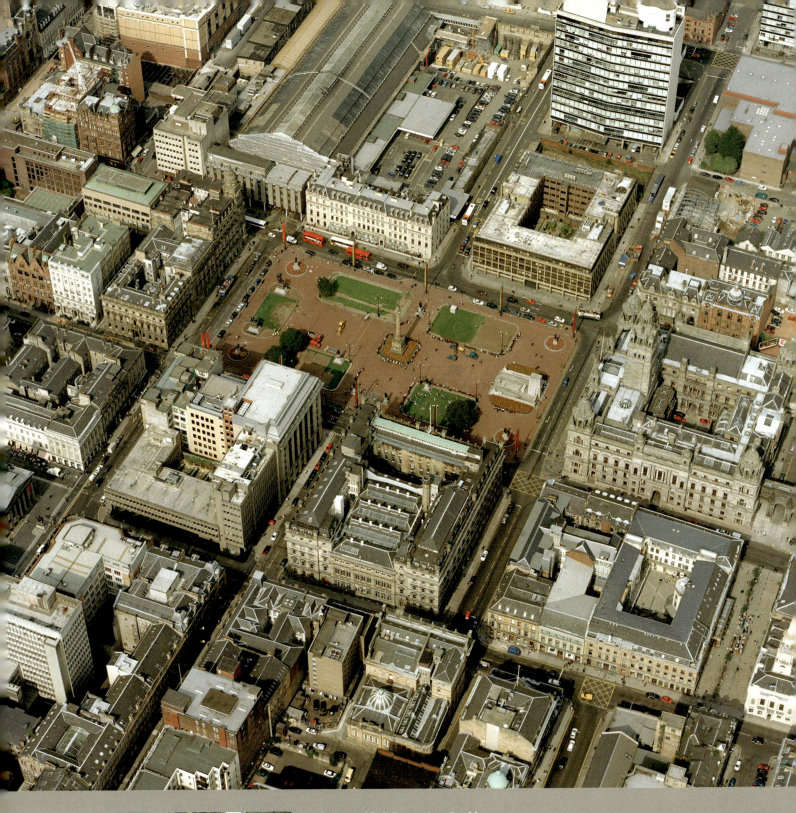

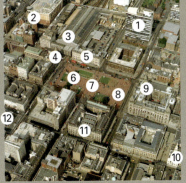

1. College of Building and Printing
2. Buchanan Galleries
3. Queen Street Station
4. Merchants' House
5. Millennium Hotel
6. George Square
7. Monument to Sir Walter Scott
8. Cenotaph
9. City Chambers
10. Hutchesons' Hall
11. General Post Office
12. Gallery of Modern Art

George Square 1998

George Square, Glasgow's civic square, is in the centre of the city and in the centre of the view. Laid out by the Town Council in 1782 it was a few years later described as 'a hollow filled with green-water and a favourite resort for drowning puppies while the banks were the slaughtering place of horses'. By 1804, two- and three-storey houses bordered the square, which was fenced off as a private garden for the householders. The square has twelve statues and as it was named in honour of King George III, the intention was to erect his statue in the centre. Sir Walter Scott stands there instead. To the right of the square is the Cenotaph with the inscription that the City of Glasgow raised 200,000 men during the First World War out of a total of more than eleven million raised in the British Empire.

Middle right in the view is the City Chambers, opened in 1888 and built to confirm Glasgow's wealth and importance as the second city of the British Empire. The style of the building is, according to the architect William Young, a 'free and dignified treatment of the Italian Renaissance'. Facing west, it fills the east side of the square, and, despite its outward appearance, it is built of bricks faced with stone. Its finest features are a 216-foot central tower and a pediment showing an enthroned Queen Victoria supported by figures representing Scotland, Ireland, England and Wales. Young based the entrance on the third-century Arch of Constantine in Rome. The interior of the building is sumptuous, with floors, walls, ceilings, balustrades and steps of marble, alabaster and mosaic.

Across the square from the City Chambers is the Merchants' House (1877), its domed tower bearing a model of a fully rigged ship atop a globe, the insignia of the House. Sharing the building is the Chamber of Commerce, founded in 1873 and the oldest in the world. Diagonally left from the City Chambers is the General Post Office. Top right, spoiling the proportions of the square, is the thirteen-storey College of Building and Printing.

Extreme top left in the view is the Buchanan Galleries shopping centre. To its right is the curved roof of Glasgow's first station, Queen Street, which, when opened in 1842, changed the status of the square, with many of the houses becoming hotels. Right of the station is the Millennium Hotel, the sole survivor of the original square as it embodies three Georgian hotels, the Queen's, the Wellington and the George.

Extreme bottom right is the white-painted Hutchesons' Hall, which terminates Hutcheson Street. Its tall, clock-faced steeple is a well-known Glasgow landmark.

An architectural drawing of Glasgow's new Municipal Buildings. Top right is the architect, William Young, a native of Paisley with a practice in London. Top left is Lord Provost Ure, who laid the foundation stone on 6 October 1883. Although the lavish interior was not finished until 1890, Queen Victoria formally opened the building in 1888.

Glasgow Caledonian University 2006

This photograph continues the view north of the previous picture. Central is Glasgow Caledonian University, the city's third university and Scotland's fourth largest. It was formed in 1993 when Queen's College and Glasgow College of Technology merged to receive university status. Since then the university has continued to grow on one city centre campus until it has become one of the most state-of-the-art university campuses in the UK. The latest addition is the Saltire Centre housing the university library; an internet-based learning café and a student services mall. The university has established a reputation for providing vocationally focused programmes and 92 per cent of its graduates seeking employment find work within six months of graduation. The university educates 98 per cent of the nurses employed by the National Health Service in Greater Glasgow and its Business School is' the largest business school in Scotland.

There is a Caledonian College of Engineering in Oman, established in 1996, where students can undertake Glasgow Caledonian University engineering programmes.

The area beyond the motorway in the top part of the view is Port Dundas, once the Glasgow terminus of the Forth and Clyde Canal. Broomhill Park is to the right of the canal. The housing below the park is that of Townhead. The group of buildings above the canal and park belongs to the Port Dundas Distillery, founded in 1820 and now owned by Diageo. To the right is North Hanover Street, forking left into Dobbies Loan. To the left is Port Dundas Road. Buchanan Bus Station is in the bottom right-hand corner.

Crown copyright RCAHMS Ref. DP9923

The Central Station Area 1930

This is an excellent view of the area around Central Station. It is so clear that the streets and their buildings are easy to identify. With the exception of some modern commercial premises, the area is largely unchanged since the photograph was taken.

Working from right to left and from south to north, the first street in the view is Glasgow's most prestigious shopping thoroughfare, Buchanan Street, which, when opened in 1780, was considered to be 'too far west' for development. When this view was taken the street ended to the north with Buchanan Street Station where trains could be caught for Oban, Perth and the north. Today it ends with the Royal Concert Hall (1987). Most of the city's best-known department stores – Fraser's, Wylie & Lochhead, Macdonalds and Wylie Hills (all gone except Fraser's) – were in Buchanan Street.

After Buchanan Street comes Mitchell Street, continuing as West Nile Street. The building with the tower in Mitchell Street is the *Glasgow Herald* Building (1893–5), Charles Rennie Mackintosh's first major project. Now called the Lighthouse, it is a centre for architecture and design. After Mitchell Street comes Union Street, continuing as Renfield Street. James Miller designed the large square building at the corner of St Vincent and Renfield Streets in classical American style for the Union Bank in 1924.

Left of Renfield Street is Hope Street, which runs from Argyle Street to Cowcaddens Road. It was originally Copenhagen Street but was changed to Hope Street in recognition of the bravery in the Peninsular War of Sir John Hope, the fourth Earl of Hopetoun. After Hope Street are Wellington and West Campbell Streets, both with a wealth of commercial buildings.

The mass between Union Street and Hope Street is the Central Station and Hotel the huge Swedish-style corner tower of which is clearly visible. The main entrance of the station fronts Gordon Street, which runs horizontally across the middle of the view between Buchanan and Hope Streets. Gordon Street was named in 1802 after Alexander 'Picture' Gordon, who bought the land opposite his new house on the east side of Buchanan Street to secure an open outlook from his windows. His nickname arose because he was the first Glasgow merchant to collect rare paintings, for which he was taunted by his fellow merchants who thought he was wasting his money which could have been more profitably invested.

The Central Station Hotel (1882–4) designed by Robert Rowand Anderson as offices for the Caledonian Railway Company but converted into a hotel after the Glasgow and South-Western Railway Company opened its St Enoch Hotel in 1879. When it opened in 1885, the luxurious Central had 550 bedrooms and accommodation for 170 servants and officials. St Enoch had only 200 bedrooms and a staff of 80. The Central's massive seventeenth-century style tower makes a handsome contribution to the junction of Gordon Street and Hope Street. Above the entrance at the corner of Gordon Street is a lion rampant, the lion being the symbol of the Caledonian Railway, which built the hotel, now called the Quality Central.
Courtesy of Glasgow Development and Regeneration Services

1. Buchanan Street
2. Mitchell Street
3. Glasgow Herald
   Building
4. West Nile Street
5. Renfield Street
6. Union Bank
   of Scotland
7. Union Street
8. Central Station
9. Hope Street
10. Wellington Street
11. West Campbell
    Street

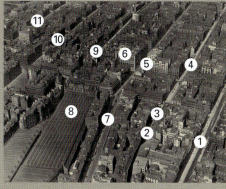

1. Kings Theatre
2. Renfield St Stephen's Church
3. Glasgow School of Art
4. St Columba (Gaelic) Parish Church
5. St Vincent Free Church
6. Blythswood Square
7. Central Station and Hotel

The Commercial Centre 1990

From the bottom upwards, three-quarters of this view covers the Commercial Centre, which stretches from Argyle Street to Sauchiehall Street and from Queen Street to the M8 motorway.

Building in the area, once known as Blythswood New Town, began at the beginning of the eighteenth century with streets such as Bath, St Vincent, West Regent and West George. While at first residential, the new town developed into a commercial centre, with the richest architectural mix in the city – Georgian buildings rubbing shoulders with impressive Victorian and Edwardian business chambers. Some modern buildings have crept in.

The description of the view starts bottom right with the Kings Theatre in Bath Street. The Glasgow Herald described its opening on 12 September 1904 as 'Brilliant'. Along from the theatre is Renfield St Stephen's Church (1849–52), which has the first of the tall spires that once dominated central Glasgow's skyline. Left in the view is Charles Rennie Mackintosh's most celebrated building, the Glasgow School of Art in Renfrew Street, built between 1897 and 1909. Particularly famous is the two-storey galleried library, the use of dark stained timber giving it a decidedly Japanese appearance.

Near centre right is St Columba (Gaelic) Parish Church (1904) in St Vincent Street. Over the door is a motto in Gaelic, *Tigh mo chridhe, tigh mo ghràidh* ('House of my heart, house of my love'). The 200-foot Gothic spire has a life-size statue of St Columba. Beyond the church is St Vincent Street Free Church (1859), Alexander 'Greek' Thomson's masterpiece. Tweed's 1872 *Guide to Glasgow and the Clyde* describes it perfectly: 'Its lofty situation gives to its raised porticoes a commanding look which in less elevated quarters the Grecian buildings miss. It stands north and south having a portico at each end. The tower is disconnected from the church.' The interior is rich and exotic, with Egyptian and Assyrian motifs in terracotta and gold.

Central in the view is Blythswood Square (1823–9),

St Vincent Street Church, Alexander Thomson's only complete surviving church. *Crown copyright RCAHMS Ref. A59840*

originally Garden Square. Its early nineteenth-century buildings face a central garden. The Royal Scottish Automobile Club occupied the whole of the square's east side from 1909 until 2005. Madeleine Smith, tried for poisoning her lover, Pierre Emile L'Angelier, lived at Number 7.

Upwards from Blythswood Square is the Central Station and Hotel, the massive tower of which is clearly visible.

Garnethill 1966

Simmons Aerofilms

This view shows a crowded Garnethill before the M8 motorway cut through it. Garnethill, or Summerhill as it was first called, developed from the 1820s. The name Garnethill came about when the earliest building, the Observatory, was opened in 1810 by Thomas Garnet, Professor of Natural Philosophy in Anderson's College.

Running full length across the lower part of the view is Sauchiehall Street, properly *Sauchie-haugh* – 'the meadow (*haugh*) of the willow trees (*sauch*)'. At the left-hand corner of the street is the Grand Hotel (1878), demolished in 1969 to make way for the M8 motorway. The Grand was one of the premier Glasgow hotels when the railway companies were building luxurious hotels next to their stations. Rooms could be had from three shillings a night, with dinner costing five shillings.

Right of the hotel is Charing Cross and the Frenchified Charing Cross Mansions, 1889–91, by J. J. Burnet. The massive red-sandstone building has a tall galleried cupola, a clock, ten sculptured figures and the Glasgow coat of arms with the motto 'Let Glasgow

Flourish'. It was the first time red sandstone was used for a building of its size. Right of the Mansions is the former Beresford Hotel, Glasgow's first skyscraper, built for visitors to the 1938 Empire Exhibition. Its red, yellow and black decor was described as 'rhubarb and custard'. The Beresford became Strathclyde University's Baird Hall of Residence and is now housing.

North of the Beresford is Scotland's first custom-built synagogue, Garnethill. Local architect John McLeod designed it in 1897 in Romanesque-cum-Byzantine style with Moorish influences. Carved above the doorway in Hebrew is Deuteronomy 32:12, which, translated into English, is 'God alone led him and there was no strange god with him'. The numerical value of the Hebrew letters used in the verse add up to the date of the foundation of the building. The synagogue is the base for Scottish Jewish archives.

A few streets behind the synagogue is Buccleuch Street where the National Trust for Scotland owns a two-room, kitchen and bathroom flat at No. 145. Known as the Tenement House, it was the home of Miss Agnes Towart from 1911 to 1965 and is virtually unchanged from her time. It gives a fascinating insight into what tenement life was like in the first half of the twentieth century.

Running vertically up the left-hand side of the view is St George's Road, leading to St George's Cross. In the gushet between St George's Road and Woodlands Road is St George's Mansions built by the City Improvement Trust. The square building in the top right-hand quarter of the picture is Stow College. Specialising in engineering, it was the city's first purpose-built further education college and was originally described as a 'Trades School'.

This view of 1987 shows just how much Garnethill had changed in twenty-one years. The inner-ring road's western interchange slashes through it. The Grand Hotel has gone, as have the buildings across from Charing Cross Mansions. The biggest change, however, is that practically everything in the top half of the picture opposite has vanished, Stow College being the only survivor.
Crown copyright RCAHMS Ref. B21498

1. Stow College
2. St George's Cross
3. St George's Road
4. St George's Mansions
5. Buccleuch Street
6. Garnethill Synagogue
7. Beresford Hotel
8. Sauchiehall Street
9. Charing Cross Mansions
10. Grand Hotel

The Gorbals

Kingston and Tradeston

Laurieston 1950

Gorbals Cross 1966

Hutchesontown 1963

Gorbals 2005

Oatlands 1950

Kingston and Tradeston

In 1650 the Town Council, in partnership with the Trades' House and Hutchesons' Hospital, bought the lands of Gorbals from Sir Robert Douglas. The lands purchased included the districts now called Kingston, Tradeston, Laurieston and Hutchesontown. The lands were not divided until 1790 when Hutchesons' Hospital received a half, and the Council and the Trades' House a quarter. The Council retained the old Gorbals village and part of Kingston. The lands received by the Trades' House and Hutcheson's Hospital became, unoriginally, Tradeston and Hutchesontown.

This view of 2005 shows Kingston to the right and Tradeston to the left. West Street divides them. Although originally residential, by 1850 both districts were completely industrialised. While Kingston has new housing fitted neatly into the infilled Kingston Dock, Tradeston is principally a district of wholesale outlets. To the right is the M8 motorway and to the left the Central Station viaduct. Above the Kingston Dock houses are the buildings of the former Scottish Cooperative Wholesale Society.

Crown copyright RCAHMS Ref. DP9525

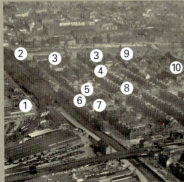

1. Tradeston
2. Jamaica Bridge
3. Carlton Place
4. South Portland Street
5. Coliseum Cinema
6. Eglinton Street
7. Bedford Cinema
8. Laurieston
9. Gorbals Parish Church
10. Gorbals Cross

Laurieston 1950

This busy photograph looks north over Laurieston, part of the lands allocated to Hutchesons' Hospital on the division of the Gorbals estate. It reached north to the Clyde, west to Bridge and Eglinton Streets, and east and south to what became Portugal and Cavendish Streets.

In 1800, the hospital feued the area to James Laurie who named it Laurieston after himself. He visualised a fashionable suburb with broad classical streets for the business and professional classes. He planned to name his streets after English nobility, and building began with Carlton Place (1802), named after the Prince Regent's London home, Carlton House.

Although the amenity of the area declined when William Dixon's horse-drawn waggonway, built to transport his coal from Little Govan Colliery to the river at Windmillquay, passed its southern edge, building continued for the professional classes until the 1840s. After that, the industrialisation of the neighbouring Tradeston reduced the status of the area and development took the form of warehouses, factories and tenements of the working-class type.

The railway viaduct running down the left-hand side of the picture divides Tradeston and Laurieston – Tradeston on the left, Laurieston on the right.

Alongside the viaduct to the right are Bridge and Eglinton Streets. Halfway up Eglinton Street are the former Coliseum and Bedford cinemas. The Coliseum opened as a music hall in 1905, became a cinema in 1925 and in 1929 showed the first 'talkie', *The Jazz Singer*, starring Al Jolson. The Coliseum is now boarded up but the Art Deco Bedford is now a concert hall named the Carling Academy.

In the photograph, Carlton Place, the most prestigious neighbourhood of Laurie's suburb, is immediately right of the south end of Jamaica Bridge. South Portland Street divides the west and east terraces. Right of Carlton Place are Gorbals Parish Church and Gorbals Cross.

Although the City Improvement Trust replaced much of the Gorbals' old overcrowded property between 1871 and 1891, many of Laurieston's earlier smarter houses remained in middle-class ownership until after 1945. Others had become teeming slums. With the exception of Carlton Place and a few buildings here and there, everything in the photograph was levelled during the 1960s' and 70s' clearances. Laurieston lost twenty-seven buildings listed as of special architectural or historic interest and today has high-rise flats and gap sites.

The impressive exterior of the category A-listed Laurieston House, which is in the centre of the east terrace of Carlton Place. The building is actually two neighbouring houses run together to look like one under a single pediment. James Laurie lived in the right-hand house, his brother David in the left. The two houses are a mirror image of each other except that the centre line is slightly offset, making the west house slightly larger. The plasterwork inside the houses is sumptuous for the time, as Georgian houses tended to be austere. The houses are presently being restored. Of the other houses in Carlton Place, the Prince and Princess of Wales Hospice occupies Nos. 71–3.

Gorbals Cross 1966

On the division of the Gorbals lands, as well as part of Kingston, the Council received the old village of Gorbals, known as far back as 1285 as Bridgend because of its proximity to the old wooden bridge over the Clyde. The church controlled the lands of Gorbals, and in 1579 Archbishop Boyd feued Bridgend to George Elphinstone who built a baronial mansion and tower in Main Street. The mansion, tower and the old chapel of St Ninian alongside survived in one form or another until the mid-nineteenth century. Gorbals was under the jurisdiction of Govan Parish until 1771.

In John McArthur's plan of Glasgow of 1778, Bridgend appears as 'Gorbells' and is shown as a few streets and a cluster of buildings arranged along lanes with vennels between them. The village extended from the Clyde on the north to today's Cumberland Street on the south, to Muirhead Street on the east and Buchan Street on the west. Weaving was the village's main industry, and there were no fewer than sixty public houses that, according to the minister, 'hurt the morals of the people not a little'.

By the second half of the nineteenth century, the old village was a crowded, crumbling slum and, along with similar properties in the city centre, the City Improvement Trust demolished it. The redeveloped area however, remained the heart of Gorbals. Main Street, leading to Victoria Bridge, was realigned and straightened, and Gorbals Cross, begun in 1872, was developed as the focal point.

This photograph shows the Victorian Gorbals village. The Cross, in the centre of the view, has corners angled to create a diamond shape. Extreme bottom right is the Citizens' Theatre (1878), originally Her Majesty's and then the Royal Princess. The building had an imposing front, with columns topped by six allegorical figures believed to have come from the Union Bank in Ingram Street. The figures were repositioned inside when the theatre received a new frontage in 1989.

Far left, in the view facing the river, is Carlton Place. To its right is the landmark spire of David Hamilton's Gorbals Parish Church of 1806, demolished in 1973. Beside the church is Gorbals Primary School. In 1885, a year after it was built, more than half the pupils were Jewish, evidence that Gorbals was the first home of a significant number of Jews in Scotland. On the right-hand side of Main Street is a bonded warehouse, originally the Adelphi Distillery, which closed in 1902.

Across the river to the right is the Fish Market with the Merchants' Steeple protruding from it. Moored beside Victoria Bridge is the clipper *Carrick*, originally the *City of Adelaide*, which was built in 1864 and conveyed countless Scots emigrants to Australia. She now lies rotting at Irvine, probably beyond restoration.

Simmons Aerofilms

This photograph of 2006 of the same area bears no relation to that of 1966. With the exception of Carlton Place and the Citizens' Theatre, everything south of the river has been demolished. The new Glasgow and Strathkelvin Sheriff Court replaces Gorbals Parish Church and Gorbals Primary School. High-rise housing replaces the tenements behind them. Glasgow's first purpose-built mosque, the Glasgow Central City Mosque (1984), which has a 162-foot-tall minaret, replaces the Adelphi Distillery. The mosque replaced a temporary building in the Gorbals that had been established in the 1940s. The intersection of Gorbals, Ballater and Norfolk Streets replaces Gorbals Cross.
Crown copyright RCAHMS Ref. DP9920

1. Citizens' Theatre
2. Gorbals Street
3. Gorbals Cross
4. Former Adelphi Distillery
5. Victoria Bridge
6. Fish Market and Merchants' Steeple
7. The Clipper Carrick
8. Buchan Street School
9. Gorbals Parish Church
10. Carlton Place

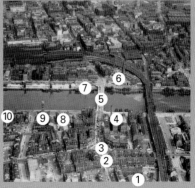

1. Cumberland Street
2. St Francis Church and Friary
3. Queen Elizabeth Square
4. Adelphi Centre
5. Laurieston
6. Tradeston

Hutchesontown 1963

Crown copyright RCAHMS Ref. DP9517-CN

Cumberland Street in the 1950s, lined with buildings and then the hub of the neighbourhood and a busy thriving shopping area.

This photograph continues the view east from the previous one on page 43 to Hutchesontown, the largest part of the land Hutchesons' Hospital received from the division of the Gorbals lands. As already mentioned, part of the Hospital's holding was developed as Laurieston.

The development in Hutchesontown on the eastern edge of Gorbals village began in 1790 to a grid plan and strict feuing conditions demanding uniform four-storey houses along streets of generous and equal width. The principal streets were Adelphi, alongside the river, and Hospital, at right angles to it. Adelphi Street was named after George and Thomas Hutcheson, founders of Hutchesons' Hospital, from the Greek word *adelphi*, meaning 'brothers'. Crown Street became the main north-south thoroughfare after the opening of the Hutchesontown Bridge, which linked it to Saltmarket. Today's bridge is the Albert, built in 1872.

Although population growth in the new suburb was initially slow, this changed when the feuers abandoned any pretensions of exclusivity and allowed the building of industrial premises. Consequently, residential streets were side-by-side with smoke-belching factories. In the 1870s tenement construction in Hutchesontown peaked, with long streets of working-class housing, mostly of one- or two-roomed flats.

By the 1930s Hutchesontown had developed into a notorious overcrowded slum, with rats the size of cats sharing space with the human population. At the beginning of the 1950s, when 87 per cent of the flats had only one or two rooms, only 3 per cent had a bath and fewer than a quarter had an inside toilet, the district was the first to be earmarked for regeneration under Glasgow Corporation's Comprehensive Development Area Plan.

When this photograph was taken, Hutchesontown was in the process of regeneration. Laurieston and Tradeston to the west were untouched. The plan was that half the houses would be twenty-storey blocks, and in the middle of the view are the Queen Elizabeth Square blocks, designed by the celebrated UK architect Sir Basil Spence. The blocks, however, were so problem-ridden that they were demolished in 1993. Tragically, a flying lump of concrete killed a local resident as they were 'blown down' during what was Europe's largest controlled explosion since the Second World War.

Dwarfed by the blocks is St Francis Church and Friary facing a cleared Cumberland Street, once Hutchesontown's main shopping street. Left and right of the view are more multistoreys. The square building to the right is the Adelphi Centre, built in 1963 as a secondary school but now a training and employment centre.

Gorbals 2005

The A-listed St Francis Church and Friary in Cumberland Street, which are descendants of Glasgow's first Franciscan friary that stood in what is now Albion Street in the city centre. This is the second church on the site. The first, of 1868, was soon too small, and the foundations of the present building, designed by Pugin and Pugin, were laid in 1880. The friary, designed by George Blount of London, was started in 1870. The church is now a community centre and the friary flats for the elderly. To the right of the church and friary are the Queen Elizabeth Square blocks that were demolished in 1993.

Although this photograph is of the area under regeneration in the previous picture, it is unrecognisable because it shows the second regeneration of Hutchesontown, now simply called Gorbals. By the 1980s, the showpiece of the 1960s had acquired an air of neglect and dilapidation. Redevelopment had tailed off, and the lack of amenities and the effects of poor building, especially the disastrous 'Hutchie E' development, were apparent. The shopping arcade in Cumberland Street was a regular haunt of drug dealers and the population had fallen to only 10,000.

In 1994 the Crown Street Regeneration Project was inaugurated with the aim of attracting people back to live in the Gorbals in rented and owner-occupied housing. With the design mistakes of the 1960s having been recognised, the emphasis was on recreating more traditional streets and more clearly defined open spaces. At the start of the project, locals were given the chance to wipe away the past by giving their area a new name. The answer was a resounding 'no'.

The area in the view has some of the UK's best contemporary residential architecture, with housing arranged around squares and lots of private and green spaces. Seventy-five per cent of the homes are owner-occupied and the rest are social rented. In 1984, only 1.2 per cent of Gorbals' housing was in private ownership.

The green area middle left in the view is the old Gorbals Parish graveyard, dating from about 1751 and now known as the Rose Garden. Some interesting gravestones remain around the walls. Beyond the graveyard is the Twomax Building (around 1816), the only survivor of Hutchesontown's industrial past and the oldest surviving iron-framed 'fireproof' mill in Glasgow. The last industrial use of the mill was in producing Twomax knitwear, the name deriving from the surnames of the two partners, McClure and McIntosh. It is now offices and studios. Above the mill is Gorbals Leisure Centre facing Ballater Street.

In the centre of the bottom half of the view is a rare nineteenth-century survivor, the former St Francis Church and Friary facing Cumberland Street. Behind them is the housing that replaced the Queen Elizabeth Square blocks shown in the previous picture. The multi-storey block extreme bottom right has now been demolished along with its companion. Curving across the middle of the view is Old Rutherglen Road.

Some residents have lived in three Gorbals – from tenements to high rises, to today's Crown Street. This regeneration is one of Glasgow's success stories. A case of third time lucky.

1. Old Gorbals Burial Ground
2. Twomax Building
3. Gorbals Leisure Centre
4. Ballater Street
5. Old Rutherglen Road
6. St Francis Church and Friary
7. Cumberland Street

1. Glasgow Green
2. River Clyde
3. Richmond Park
4. Oatlands
5. Rutherglen Road
6. Caledonia Road
7. Hutchesontown
8. Southern Necropolis
9. Govan Iron Works Coke Oven
10. Govanhill
11. Govan Iron Works

Oatlands 1950

Crown copyright RCAHMS PFFO 540/A/473 0362

Southeast of Hutchesontown is the youngest area of the Gorbals, Oatlands. It was first feued around 1870 and had a population large enough by 1877 to warrant the opening of its own sub-post office. Oatlands began east of the Southern Necropolis and ended at Polmadie Road. The neat rows of Oatlands' tenements are bottom left in the view. During regeneration, buildings in Hutchesontown were destroyed, whether crumbling or sound, while those in Oatlands were retained and renovated. Unfortunately this was short term as they were later demolished. Regeneration of the area is under way.

Diagonally bisecting the view is Oatlands' main street, Rutherglen Road, in the 1950s a bustling thoroughfare lined with shops and houses. Right of Rutherglen Road, which continues west as Caledonia Road, is Richmond Park, opened by Glasgow Corporation in 1899 to provide an open space on the south side of the river to meet the needs of the southeastern districts of Polmadie and Hutchesontown. The model-yacht sailing pond, now home to a colony of swans, was the largest of any city park. Polmadie footbridge links the park to Glasgow Green. Adjoining the park to the west was a little park known as 'the Sandy' where children could make sandcastles. Beyond that is the bowling green, established around 1900 and still going strong.

Hutchesontown's lines of streets appear in the top right-hand quarter of the view. To their left in Caledonia Road is the Southern Necropolis, opened in 1840 and Glasgow's first attempt to provide the working person with the opportunity for a cheap but dignified burial. At the time the lower classes could hope for little more than burial in a mass or common grave. Glasgow architect Charles Wilson designed the massive castellated arched gateway in 1848. Among those of note buried in the graveyard are Gorbals-born Sir Thomas Lipton, grocer, yachtsman and millionaire. Also there are architect Alexander 'Greek' Thomson and engineer John Robertson who designed the engines for the steamship *Comet*.

Near the centre of the view is Govan Iron Works, founded in 1839 by William Dixon and popularly known as Dixon's Blazes as its five blast furnaces cast a great red glow that illuminated the night sky over the Gorbals and Govanhill. The works closed down in 1959 and the site became Dixon's Blazes Industrial Estate. The left upper part of the picture shows Govanhill, developed by William Dixon's son in the 1870s to house his workers, who had the best working-class housing in Britain, with internal sanitation and at least two rooms. Fortunately, unlike in the Gorbals where practically everything was swept away, Govanhill's tenements were renovated, and today it is the most intact of Glasgow's Victorian working-class suburbs.

Rutherglen Road, Oatlands, in the 1960s. As the photograph shows, the tenements lining the road, with shops underneath, had become rundown. Today, none of them remains as they were demolished to make way for the regeneration of the area now under way.

The North Side

Ruchill Park

This view of 2006 shows Ruchill Park and the remainder of Ruchill Hospital, both built simultaneously on the estate of Roughill, purchased by the Corporation in 1891. The park, top in the view, opened in 1892. Its tremendous views over Glasgow were emphasised by an artificial mound known locally as Ben Whitton, after the then Director of Parks, James Whitton, who had it formed from 24,000 cartloads of waste material from the building of the hospital. Spion Kop, adopted from a Boer War engagement, is another name for the mound.

Ruchill Hospital for Infectious Diseases opened in 1900, and prominent in the view is its A-listed water tower, necessary because of the high ground on which the hospital was built. A housing development is planned for the grounds and remaining hospital buildings. Top left in the view is the Forth and Clyde Canal. *Crown copyright RCAHMS Ref: DP9916*

Maryhill 2005

This picture shows a troop inspection in 1903 at Maryhill Barracks, built to replace the old ones in Gallowgate. The new barracks had accommodation for a regiment of infantry, a squadron of cavalry and a battery of field artillery. There were officers' quarters, three two-storey blocks for married men and four three-storey blocks for single soldiers. There was also a chapel, a hospital and a prison. A detachment from the 6th Dragoons were the first troops to occupy the barracks.

Maryhill Barracks.   RELIABLE SERIES

Crown copyright RCAHMS Ref. DP9582

Maryhill owes its existence to the Forth and Clyde Canal. Previously, it was an area of rural estates, one of them, Gairbraid, owned by Mary Hill, who married Robert Graham in 1763. The couple had no income other than from the estate, and to create wealth Robert tried sinking coal pits, a venture that proved profitless. The winds of change blew their way, however, when Parliament approved the cutting of the Forth and Clyde Canal through their estate. They had hit the jackpot.

Starting from the River Forth in 1768, the canal reached Stockingfield (Maryhill) in 1775 and Hamiltonhill (on the outskirts of the city) in 1777 when work stopped because of lack of funds. Construction recommenced in 1785 with the building of the magnificent four-arched aqueduct over the River Kelvin, five locks and a dry dock. The 39-lock canal, with a collateral cut to Port Dundas, reached Bowling on the Clyde in 1790. It was the world's first coast-to-coast ship canal, and the first ship to travel the thirty-five mile waterway was the Leith-built *Agnes*.

When a village developed around the dry dock, the Grahams feued land to expand it on condition that it was to be 'in all times called the town of Mary Hill'. Previously it was known as Drydock, Kelvindock or simply the Dock. A canalside sawmill at the dock was nicknamed 'Maryhill Cathedral' when the Free Kirk met in it after the Disruption in the Church of Scotland of 1843.

As the canal traffic grew, so did Maryhill, and by 1850 it had a population of 3,000 and industries such as boat building, paper mills, sawmills, foundries, chemical plants and glass factories. Murano Street, overlooking the canal, was named after the Italian city of Venice's main glass manufactory.

Winding its way across the view is the canal, with the five Maryhill Locks and their holding basins on the right. From the right, between the third and fourth locks, is the former dry dock. Right of the locks is the River Kelvin, flowing towards Kelvinside, top right in the view.

Extreme middle left in the view is Lochburn Park, the ground of Maryhill Football Club, founded in 1884 and the oldest junior club in the north side of Glasgow. It was the Central League Champion 1997–98 and greats such as Danny McGrain and Tommy Burns came from its ranks.

Right of the football park is the Wyndford Housing Estate, built on the site of Maryhill Barracks, which opened in 1876 and over the years housed various regiments before becoming the headquarters of the Highland Light Infantry in 1920. When the barracks were demolished in 1961, in the face of local opposition, the wall and guardhouse were retained.

1. Kelvinside
2. River Kelvin
3. Maryhill Locks
4. Former Dry Dock
5. Forth and Clyde Canal
6. Lochburn Park
7. Maryhill Road
8. Wyndford Housing Estate

Maryhill Locks 2002

This amazing view of the Forth and Clyde Canal's spectacular Maryhill Locks was shot from a balloon. It shows four of the five locks and their holding basins. The locks, numbers 25 to 21, raise the canal's level by about 40 feet. Behind the third basin is the former dry dock of 1789. Among its occupants was the Swan family, who from 1837 to 1893 built iron ships in sections some of which were then assembled in Bowling. The Swans built the *Glasgow* in 1857, the first of the well-known 'puffers', so nicknamed from the noise of their exhaust exiting through the funnel. Between the 1860s and 1921, the yard built around sixty puffers. It closed in 1962.

The death knell of the Forth and Clyde Canal began to sound with the opening of the Edinburgh and Glasgow Railway in 1842. For passengers and freight, the train was more practical, and in 1867 the Caledonian Railway bought the canal company, largely to acquire the port of Grangemouth as an outlet on the Forth. Thereafter the canal struggled on, but when the Admiralty closed the Forth ports to civilian shipping during the First World War, it went into a decline and eventually closed in 1962. It lay derelict for a generation, but then, thanks to a huge grant from the Millennium Commission, navigation was restored to the whole of the Forth and Clyde Canal, with a ceremonial re-opening on 26 May 2001. This view shows the restored Maryhill Locks which, along with the Kelvin Aqueduct, are scheduled ancient monuments. *Courtesy of Hawkeye Photography*

Forth and Clyde Canal, Firhill Basin and Firhill Park 1998

This view shows a floodlit match between Partick Thistle and Clydebank on 8 October 1991. The score was Partick Thistle 0, Clydebank 3.
Courtesy of Partick Thistle

This view shows the Firhill Basin of the Forth and Clyde Canal, with Firhill Park, the home of Partick Thistle Football Club, behind it. The basin, constructed in 1788 by widening a bend in the canal with a second basin made on the inside of the bend in 1849, was originally a pond for seasoning timber. Big logs were left floating in the water to keep them moist while they aged, and children were always being warned about the dangers of playing on the logs. Extreme middle left in the view is a stop lock added during the Second World War. If, during air raids, the canal's bank was breached and water poured out, the lock could be closed, preventing too much water escaping. Luckily, the canal escaped harm.

Partick Thistle, popularly known as the 'Jags' and founded in 1876, has been described as 'the friendly team' and 'the thinking man's alternative to Celtic and Rangers'. Before settling in Maryhill in 1909, the club had several homes, starting with public ground at what is now the site of the Art Galleries. Its fifth park was in Partick, at Meadowside on the banks of the Clyde, and it was said that two men in a rowing boat were stationed on the river to retrieve wandering balls. When the club had to move to make way for riverside devel-

opment, it was to Firhill, an out-of-the-way district to the north of Glasgow. Until the ground was completed, home matches were played at Ibrox Park.

Thistle's successes have been limited, its most notable being winning the Scottish Cup in 1921 by beating Rangers 1–0. The venue for the game was Celtic Park. *The Evening News'* editorial observed: 'The big clubs cannot have it all their own way. The winning of the Scottish Cup by Partick Thistle has restored to professional sport the essential element of the unexpected.' The next highlight came fifty years later, in 1971, when Thistle beat Celtic 4–1 at Hampden to win the League Cup. The season 1997–98 was disastrous as the club was relegated to Division Two. Presently it is in Division One. While crowds today are not huge, in 1922 a match against Rangers at Firhill attracted 49,838 people.

Although the Jags are not one of Scottish football's big guns, their red-brick and roughcast building is a landmark. The stand nearest the canal was built in 1994 and named after Jackie Husband, a well-known pre-Second World War player famed for the length of his throw-ins.

1. Forth and Clyde Canal
2. Firhill Timber Basin
3. Stop Lock
4. Jackie Husband Stand
5. Firhill Road

1. The Saracen Foundry
2. Saracen Street
3. Saracen Cross
4. Balmore Road
5. Mecca Cinema
6. Firhill Basin of Forth and Clyde Canal
7. Westercommon
8. Hamiltonhill

Possilpark 1950

The Forth and Clyde Canal reached Lambhill in 1774 and Hamiltonhill in 1777, and while industry centred on these northern and southern parts of Possil, the area in between remained rural until well into the nineteenth century. There was not even a village, just some small farms, quarries, coal pits and a few rows of workers' cottages.

All this changed when Walter Macfarlane, the owner of the Saracen Foundry in Anderston, originally in Saracen Street, off Gallowgate, bought Possil House and its estate in 1869. Previously, Sir Archibald Alison, Sheriff of Glasgow, had rented it. Among his visitors was Charles Dickens, who called Possil the 'Garden of the North . . . a relief from the general deprivation in Glasgow.' Apparently, Alison, who had written a forty-volume History of Europe, had told Dickens that he had no future as a novelist and should try some other field of literary activity.

After demolishing Possil House and felling the trees, Macfarlane erected a foundry on part of the site and streets and houses for his workforce on the rest, creating the new community of Possilpark. Saracen Street led directly north to the intricate, cast-iron foundry gates.

The foundry, bottom left in the view, manufactured domestic, ornamental and architectural ironwork, and while much of its exported work has survived, Glasgow has few remaining examples. Of these, the best is in Macfarlane's former home at 22 Park Circus, the carriage canopy in front of Central Station and the fountain in Alexandra Park. A small fountain in the heart of Possil bears the words 'Keep the Pavement Dry'.

After the Saracen, other iron works arrived, along with industries such as pottery, chemicals and steel. None of these survived the 1960s, changing Possilpark from a high-wage area to one of deprivation. The Saracen closed in 1965, and the site is now an urban garden and play area.

Behind the foundry, divided by Saracen Street, are tenements built by Macfarlane for his workers. The larger building right of the foundry in Balmore Road is the Mecca Cinema, opened in 1933, renamed the Vogue after the Second World War and now a bingo hall. Saracen Cross at the junction of Saracen Street and Balmore Road was the meeting place for local residents. Its central feature was a Macfarlane clock tower and fountain trough.

Right of the view is the Firhill Basin of the Forth and Clyde Canal, with left of it the Westercommon, all that is left of Glasgow's once extensive common lands. Left of the common is Hamiltonhill, a housing estate of the 1930s.

The Saracen Foundry showroom in 1890 demonstrating the wide range of its products. At the time, the company was world famous, with a 2,000-page two-volume catalogue listing 6,000 items including everything from rainwater pipes, gutters, baths and street lamps to conservatories, fountains and bandstands. While parks worldwide still have Macfarlane fountains and bandstands, Glasgow Corporation scrapped most of theirs in the 1960s, insisting they were too expensive to maintain.

Port Dundas 1960

Crown copyright P.543/RAF/996 0151

In 1790 the Glasgow branch of the Forth and Clyde Canal was extended from Hamiltonhill to Hundred Acre Hill (owned by Mary Hill) where a new terminal was created and named Port Dundas after Sir Lawrence Dundas, governor of the canal company. In 1791, a cut of junction was made to the Monkland Canal, giving Port Dundas access to a large supply of water and an extension to trade routes.

A pleasant village grew up around Port Dundas, but, attracted to its nearness to the city centre, industry and commerce moved in, making it Glasgow's most important port as ship owners often preferred to bring their vessels up to the city by canal as ships could be stranded at low tide at the Broomielaw. Trade coming into Port Dundas from the east was more than double the combined total of trade with the Clyde and that going to the Forth. When further basins were added, Port Dundas became industrialised, with foundries, chemical and dye works, distilleries, engine works, grain mills and sugar refineries.

This view shows Port Dundas before most of the basin had disappeared under the M8 motorway. Prominent is the massive cooling tower of Pinkston Power Station, built in 1901 to supply power for the electrification of the city's tramcar system. The power station and the tower, built 1952–4 and the largest in Europe at the time, were demolished in the 1970s.

Across the canal from the tower, in North Canal-bank Street, is the conglomeration of the Port Dundas Distillery and bottling plant, founded in 1820 and said to be the first Scottish distillery to use imported grain after the repeal of the Corn Laws in 1846. Now owned by Diageo, the distillery has been blending and bottling whisky since the 1890s, including the famous White Horse brand.

On the left of the view, fronting the canal, is North Spiers Wharf, which once housed the Port Dundas Sugar Refinery and the City of Glasgow Grain Mills and Stores. The Canal Offices of 1812 are also there. In the forefront and right-hand corner of the view is Cowcaddens, now cut off from the canal by the M8 motorway. In the 1860s it was one of the most polluted and densely populated areas in Glasgow, and a map of the time shows how industry, such as soap, dye and asphalt works, was freely mixed with housing. Sighthill Cemetery and the soda wastes created by the St Rollox Chemical Works are across the top.

North Spiers Wharf, once a very busy place on the canal that became rundown when the canal closed. This photograph shows the long range of Victorian white sandstone grain mills and stores restored and converted into offices and houses. To their right is the Georgian Canal Offices building. The view from the wharf over Glasgow is magnificent as the basin is built on a prominent platform. Work is under way to turn Port Dundas into a canal quarter to rival London's Little Venice, with a stunning waterfall feature, offices, housing, and leisure facilities. Once completed the area will be renamed Spier Locks.

1. North Spiers Wharf
2. Forth and Clyde Canal
3. Port Dundas Distillery
4. Sighthill Cemetery
5. Soda Wastes
6. Pinkston Power Station and Cooling Tower
7. Cowcaddens
8. Dundashill Distillery

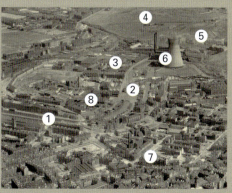

1. The Monkland Canal
2. St Joseph's Home for the Elderly
3. Townhead and Blochairn Parish Church
4. St Roch's Secondary School
5. St Rollox Railway Works
6. Castle Street

Royston 1950

East of Port Dundas is Royston, once called Garngad but rechristened by the Corporation in 1942 in an attempt to obliterate the memory of a district notorious for being an insanitary overcrowded industrial slum.

Starting with Charles Tennant's famous St Rollox Chemical Works, where bleaching powder and sulphuric acid were manufactured, heavy industry developed in Garngad after the opening of the Monkland Canal in 1790. Built as a means of bringing coal into Glasgow from the rich coalfields around Coatbridge, the Monkland Canal ended at Townhead before linking with the Forth and Clyde Canal at Port Dundas in 1790.

By 1860 the industrial explosion had begun to swallow up the area and to accommodate the huge workforce poor quality tenement housing was built on and around Garngad Road and Garngardhill. There have been several slum clearance schemes in the Garngad area. One scheme, 'Houses for Heroes' in 1918–20, saw the building of Garngad Square. Another scheme in the 1930s swept away many of the nineteenth-century tenements.

Industry, including the chemical works, remained in Royston until the 1960s when the M8 motorway (constructed on the foundations of the Monkland Canal and the cut of the junction with the Forth and Clyde) and new housing swept it away. Among the new housing were tower blocks, five in Charles Street and three in Millburn Street, one of which had to be demolished in 1992 because of spiralling maintenance costs.

This view shows Royston and the Monkland Canal before the 1960s' clearance. The canal runs across the front of the view with Townhead below it. Middle right is Townhead and Blochairn Parish Church built in 1865–6 on Royston Hill. Its extremely tall tower, all that is left of the church, is a well-known landmark. Right of the church is St Joseph's Home for the Elderly, opened by the Little Sisters of the Poor in 1864. Private housing known as St Joseph's View is now on the site.

Left of the church are Victorian tenements that escaped the 1930s' clearance. Behind the church is 1930s' housing among which, to the left, is the E-shaped St Roch's Secondary School, opened in 1928 and built on the site of the old Glasgow Malleable Iron Works.

Left in the view near the top are the St Rollox Railway Works built for the Caledonian Railway Company, which became part of the London Midland and Scottish Railway in 1923, which in turn became part of British Railways in 1948. Regardless of any name change, however, the works were always known as 'The Caley'.

A view from the west of Townhead and Blochairn Parish Church, now demolished except for the tower, a landmark on the hill above the M8 motorway which separates the church from Townhead as had the Monkland Canal. Right of the church is one of the tower blocks erected when the council declared Royston a Comprehensive Redevelopment Area in 1964. *Crown copyright RCAHMS Ref. A43139*

Blochairn and Riddrie 2005

Hogganfield Loch and grounds at the beginning of the 1970s. At that time Hogganfield was the mecca of many Glasgow families who brought their children out to what seemed like the country. There was plenty of open space to sit and enjoy the scenery, enhanced by the waters of the loch. People could take a trip on a motor boat, hire a rowing boat or play pitch and putt on the course beside the tearoom.

Neighbouring Royston is Blochairn, with Blackhill and Riddrie farther east. The Monkland Canal ran through the districts towards its terminus at Calderbank.

Alongside the M8 motorway are two vivid blue gasholders, 280 feet in diameter, that belong to Provan Gas Works, begun in 1900 for Glasgow Corporation Gas Department, which became the Scottish Gas Board, Glasgow Division, in 1949. To the right of the holders is Alexandra Park and in front of them the bus station and brick works. Bottom right is part of the large complex that houses the Fruit, Vegetable and Fish markets. The Fish Market moved from Bridgegate in 1977 and the Fruit and Vegetable Market was originally in the Candleriggs. The site of today's markets once housed Blochairn Steelworks. Glasgow's biggest car boot sale is held beside the markets every weekend. Royston Road is to the left of the view.

Public housing began to spread across the countryside in 1920, and in the top right-hand quarter of the view is Riddrie, the Corporation's first scheme. Previously the area had been open countryside and farmland. In the centre of the section is Barlinnie Prison, the only prison within the city's boundaries and popularly known as the 'Bar-L'. When it opened in 1882, it had room for 1,000 prisoners. In 1928, executions were transferred from Duke Street Prison to Barlinnie, the last being in 1960 when nineteen-year-old Anthony Miller was hanged, he and a youth having been convicted of battering a man to death while robbing him. Scotland's most notorious serial murderer, Peter Manual, was hanged at Barlinnie on 11 July 1958.

Across the motorway from Riddrie is Blackhill, a slum clearance scheme of the 1930s to which tenants from the old Garngad slums were moved. When the canal was filled in and became part of the M8 motorway, it took away much of Blackhill, which had been almost as famous for its canal locks as Maryhill.

Top left in the view is Hogganfield Loch, the source of the Molendinar Burn, which eventually emptied into the River Clyde at the Tidal Weir below Albert Bridge. When the park around the loch opened in 1924, special provision was made for boating, and as the loch extends for fifty-three acres, motor and rowing boats were in great demand. There is no longer boating on the loch, fed by five springs from the Ruchazie side of the grounds. The island in the centre of the loch is a bird sanctuary, and since 1968 the park has been a local nature reserve.

1. Hogganfield Loch and Park
2. Blackhill
3. Riddrie
4. Barlinnie Prison
5. M8 Motorway
6. Alexandra Park
7. Gas-holders
8. Fruit, Vegetable and Fish Markets

1. St Rollox Railway Works
2. Springburn Road
3. Sighthill Cemetary
4. Cowlairs Railway Works
5. Hydepark Locomotive Works
6. Atlas Locomotive Works

Springburn Locomotive Works 1947

Crown copyright CPE/SCOT/UK/277 5045

Glasgow's greatest heavy industry next to shipbuilding was locomotive engineering. Springburn was its centre, and this vertical view shows all four of its works. Using the names current at the time the view was taken, they are: the London Midland and Scottish (LMS) at St Rollox, the London and North Eastern Railways (LNER) at Cowlairs and the North British Locomotive Company's Hydepark and Atlas Works.

Middle left is the North British Railway Company's Cowlairs Works, established in 1841 by the Edinburgh and Glasgow Railway and taken over in 1865 by the North British. After the works became part of LNER in 1923, they ceased locomotive building but continued to maintain and repair them. Cowlairs became part of British Railways in 1948, and in 1966 it closed, a casualty of Dr Beeching's cuts.

Middle bottom in the view, on the right of Springburn Road, are the London Midland and Scottish works, which began in 1854 as the Caledonian Railway Company's St Rollox Works. Within the site was the Glasgow and Garnkirk line of 1831, which operated Scotland's first passenger service. St Rollox built, maintained and repaired locomotives, coaches and goods wagons, but after becoming part of LMS in 1923, it concentrated on maintenance and repair work. The LMS became part of British Railways in 1948 and later British Rail Engineering Ltd. In 1990, the works, always known as the 'Caley' despite the name changes, closed.

In the middle of the view are the North British Locomotive Company's Hydepark and Atlas Works, separated by railway tracks, Hydepark to the left, Atlas to the right. To meet American competition, the NBL was formed in 1903 by the amalgamation of three of Glasgow's locomotive builders, Sharp Stewart of Atlas Works, Neilson Reid of Hydepark Works and Henry Dubs of Glasgow Locomotive Works at Polmadie. After the amalgamation, it became the largest firm of locomotive builders in Europe, with 8,000 employees.

The NBL exported most of its production to Africa,

This advertisement of 1931 for the North British Locomotive Company shows that it produced locomotives for the home market as well as exporting them worldwide. The first of the famous Royal Scots was completed on 14 July 1927.

South America, India and the Far East, and it was an impressive sight to see 80-ton locomotives pulled out of the works by horses or steam traction engines into Vulcan Street and then down Springburn Road on their way to the docks at Finnieston to be shipped worldwide.

As the company failed to successfully make the transition from steam to diesel, it closed in 1962.

Springburn 1950

In the days before industry came to it, Springburn was a scattered rural hamlet inhabited by weavers, miners and farm and quarry workers. Dotted around were farms and the country houses of Glasgow's merchants and gentry. The spring from which the village took its name arose on Balgray Hill, from where it splashed down the slopes before joining the burn flowing from Petershill Loch, lying in the vicinity of today's Flemington Street. Like Rome, Springburn is built on seven hills – Balgrayhill, Barnhill, Keppochhill, Petershill, Sighthill, Stobhill and Springburnhill, the most closely associated with the original village. Springburn was always part of Glasgow, unlike other villages annexed by the city.

Bottom middle in the view is Sighthill Cemetery, laid out in 1840. It occupies a sloping position and rises to a height of nearly 400 feet above sea level. On the main avenue is the Martyrs' Memorial commemorating Andrew Hardie and John Baird, leaders of the 'Radical Rising' of 1820, who were executed at Stirling Castle for treason. Added later was the name of James Wilson, executed at Glasgow on the same charge.

Alongside the cemetery is the former Corporation Tram Depot and electricity generating station, built in 1898 for the experimental electrification of the Mitchell Street to Springburn route. The Springburn Steam Laundry took over one of the sheds in 1904 while another became the Oxford Cinema in 1927. To the right of the cemetery, on Springburn Road, is Sighthill Church, which disappeared, along with the housing around it and the cemetery, when the construction of the A803 in the 1970s split Springburn in half.

Middle right in the view are the Atlas locomotive works, with the Hydepark works to their left. All that remains of both works is the quadrangle to the right of them, the magnificent red sandstone Hydepark administration building of 1908 in Flemington Street, now occupied by North Glasgow College. Outside, sculptures represent science and speed, and over the door is a superb carving of a locomotive. The building is so impressive internally that it has a heritage trail. Behind the magnificent wood and marble staircase are windows containing striking stained glass First World War memorials.

Across the top of the view are Springburn Park, Stobhill Hospital and Balornock, which feature in the next view.

With the exception of the cemetery, the former tram depot, a few houses, and the Hydepark administration building, this view of 1991 is unrecognisable from that of 1950. The motorway that split the district in half has swept the rest away. Top right is the shopping centre of 1980, which replaced dozens of tenements and shops. Left of the centre is St Aloysius RC Church of 1888, a survivor of the district's obliteration and now Springburn's oldest church building. *Crown copyright RCAHMS Ref. B71325*

1. Former Corporation Tram Depot
2. Sighthill Cemetery
3. Sighthill Church
4. Hydepark Administration Building
5. Hydepark Works
6. Atlas Works
7. Balornock
8. Springburn Park
9. Stobhill Hospital

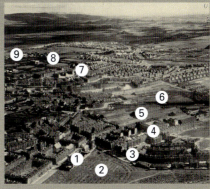

1. Campsie Street
2. Albert Secondary School
3. Broomfield Road
4. Springburn Park
5. Amphitheatre Bandstand
6. Water Tower
7. Stobhill Hospital
8. Littlehill Golf Course
9. Menzies Road, Drive and Place
10. Drumbottie Road

Balornock, Springburn Park and Stobhill Hospital 1950

This view of Springburn Park shows the Winter Garden, erected in 1900 and affectionately known as the 'Hothouses'. Four wings extend from the main structure, which originally held tropical trees and ferns but later became an exhibition area where shows and concerts were performed. The viewing gallery displayed the finest floral displays in the country. Because of fire damage and vandalism, the Winter Garden was closed in the mid-1980s and now lies in ruins.

Balornock is a large Corporation housing scheme begun in the 1920s and continued in the 1960s when it involved the destruction of the Victoria 'villadom' of Balgrayhill, the desirable part of Springburn.

Anyone living in the part of north Balornock shown in the view will be able to spot their houses, as streets such as Broomfield, Drumbottie and Campsie are clearly visible. The oval to the right contains Menzies Road, Drive and Place. To the left, in Mansell Street, is the E-shaped Albert Secondary School of 1926–27.

Behind the school is Springburn Park, laid out in 1892 on the crown of Balgrayhill. When the park was acquired it was a windswept piece of mediocre agricultural land with the remains of an ironstone pit in one corner and a disused quarry in another.

As the highest point in the park is 351 feet above sea level the view from there is spectacular, encompassing Ben Lomond, Loch Katrine and the Trossachs.

Because of the steepness of Balgrayhill, Springburn was the only Glasgow park that did not have a tramcar service to its gates. Extreme middle left in the view is the amphitheatre-style bandstand that replaced the original ornamental cast-iron one manufactured at the nearby Saracen Foundry in Possilpark and gifted by James Reid of Hydepark locomotive fame. Alongside is the cricket ground (now open parkland), with the football ground to its right. The oblong building is a water reservoir, a landmark for miles around.

Behind the park is Stobhill Hospital, planned in 1899 as a Poor Law Hospital to supplement the Barony Poorhouse at Barnhill. Stobhill, with 1,867 beds contained in twenty-eight two-storey pavilions, opened in 1904. It became a general hospital in 1929. A multimillion pound state-of-the-art hospital is to replace the old buildings. Right of the hospital is Littlehill Golf Course, the longest of the public 18-hole golf courses and created on land gifted by the Reid family.

Red Road Multistorey Flats 2006

Crown copyright RCAHMS Ref. DP9908

Multistorey house building developed because of a scarcity of land. It was also felt that tenants in tenements were used to the idea of living upstairs without a garden to look at. The designation of a multistorey house was one served by a lift. Broadcaster Jimmy Reid called them 'filing cabinets for people'.

This view shows the Red Road multistorey blocks in south Balornock, notorious for their height, cost and problems. (Red Road runs horizontally across the middle of the view.) Designed for the Corporation in 1962 by Sam Bunton & Associates, the blocks were, according to Mr Bunton, 'public building without airs and graces'. Consisting of two 26–28-storey blocks, four point blocks and two tower blocks of 31 storeys, they were reputedly the highest residential blocks in Europe.

The development housed nearly 4,700 people, the population of a small town that would have had its own local services run by a council. The blocks had a mixture of two, three and four apartments, and although the flats were comfortable and offered splendid views for miles around, building economies meant that there was a deficiency of communal facilities and lifts. Those lifts that there were often did not work, leaving unfit tenants stranded. In 1980, because of vandalism, two of the blocks were deemed unfit for habitation. The red, blue and ochre cladding added to the blocks in 1982 gave them a much needed uplift. There are plans to demolish the Red Road flats along with other high-rise blocks in the city.

To the left in the view behind the flats is Petershill Road. On its left is an industrial estate and on its right houses built on the site of Foresthill Hospital, originally Barnhill Poorhouse, built in 1853 for the indoor treatment of all sane poor. Discipline in Barnhill was strict, and able-bodied inmates who did not meet their work quota were put on a diet of bread and water in solitary confinement for twelve hours. Barnhill was renamed Foresthall House and Hospital in 1945. Right of the former hospital is the Barnhill area of Springburn.

This photograph of a Red Road multistorey block in the 1980s shows just how rundown the estate had become.

1. Broomfield Road
2. Red Road
   Multistorey Flats
3. Red Road
4. Petershill Road
5. Former Foresthill
   Hospital Site

The South Side

The Burrell Gallery

This view of 2005 shows the building that houses the
Burrell Collection, the priceless collection of works of art
bequeathed to the city by Sir William Burrell in 1944. As
Burrell had specified that the collection was to be sited no
fewer than sixteen miles from the Royal Exchange, away
from Glasgow's noxious atmosphere, it took three decades
to choose the present site in Pollok Park, the largest green
belt enclosed within any city in the world and gifted to
Glasgow by the Maxwell family. Opened in 1983, the
Burrell building, largely of glass, stainless steel and pink
Dumfries-shire stone, took twelve years to design and
construct. It reaches to the edge of the woodland, and only
glass walls separate the trees from the gallery, bringing the
outside in. *Crown copyright RCAHMS Ref. DP9902*

1. White's Chemical Works
2. Shawfield Stadium
3. Richmond Park
4. Oatlands
5. Hutchesontown
6. Southern Necropolis
7. Govan Iron Works
8. Caledonian Mineral and Goods Depot
9. Queen's Park Locomotive Works
10. Polmadie Motive Power Depot
11. Barrage Ballooons

Wartime View of Southeast Glasgow 1941

As this superb view of the southeast area of the city was taken during the Second World War, careful scrutiny will reveal barrage balloons dotted about. The River Clyde snakes down the right-hand side of the view, with Bridgeton centre right and Glasgow Green within the deep curve.

Bottom right in Rutherglen is White's Chemical Works, founded in 1810. By 1840, its main product was bichromate of potash, originally used for dyes. This product led to a medical condition known as chrome holes – many workers could put a hankie up one nostril and pull it out the other because of cartilage damage caused by chemical fumes. Although the works closed down in the 1960s its legacy remains, with untreated chromium waste still contaminating the Rutherglen-Cambuslang area.

Above White's Works is Shawfield Stadium, once the home of Clyde Football Club, the 'Bully Wee', who won the Scottish Cup in 1939 and kept it for seven years, a record at the time. Part of the stadium is in Rutherglen and part in Glasgow. It is an oft-repeated story that at one end of the stadium you could score a goal in Rutherglen and at the other end you could score one in Glasgow. A barrage balloon is right of the stadium, which is now Shawfield Greyhound Stadium.

Richmond Park, with a barrage balloon in its centre, is left of the stadium. Left of Richmond Park is Oatlands, along from which is the Southern Necropolis with the serried rows of Hutcheson-town's tenements to its right.

Behind the Necropolis are the Govan Iron Works, founded in 1839 by William Dixon and popularly known as Dixon's Blazes as the early blast furnaces had no tops and flames would soar up from the inside, lighting the night sky over the Gorbals and Govanhill. It was the last blast foundry to operate within the city boundary and it closed down in 1959.

Left of the Caledonian Goods and Mineral Depot is the Queen's Park Locomotive Works, opened in 1864 by German engineer Henry Dubs. In 1905, when the company was the second largest builder of steam engines in the country and employed 2,423 men, it merged with the Atlas and Hyde Park Works in Springburn to form the North British Locomotive Company. All three works closed in 1963. Left of the locomotive works is Govanhill, once a police burgh within Lanarkshire but annexed to Glasgow in 1891.

The bleak ground in the bottom quarter of the view is Polmadie, where a barrage balloon is visible.

This drawing by William Simpson of the late 1840s shows the five open-top blast furnaces of the Govan Iron Works as well as a row of cottages built for the employees of William Dixon's Little Govan Colliery.

Hampden Park 2006

Hampden Park was the world's first international football stadium. Surprisingly, however, given its status in the professional game, it was built for an amateur side, Queen's Park.

There have been three Hampden Parks, the one in the view being the third with a new stadium built on it. The first, situated alongside Prospecthill Road, was opened by Queen's Park in 1873 and called Hampden after the terrace opposite, named after John Hampden, a seventeenth-century English Parliamentarian. So, ironically, Hampden, that bastion of Scottish national pride, was named after an Englishman.

Queen's Park had to abandon its ground in 1873 when plans showed that the Cathcart Circle train line would cut through it. By 1884, however, the club had relocated to the east side of Cathcart Road and had a second Hampden, a nice little stadium with a main stand, brick pavilion and gym. However, as the club only leased the ground, it paid £10,000 in 1900 for a site in Somerville Drive in Mount Florida that became the third Hampden Park. (Third Lanark took over the second Hampden and re-christened it Cathkin Park.)

The third Hampden Park consisted of three sides of terracing and two south stands with nothing in between. There were no dressing rooms and the players and officials had to change in a flat rented by the club at 113 Somerville Drive. The opening game was on 31 October 1903 when Queen's Park beat Celtic 1–0. The first international was on 7 April 1906, when Scotland beat England 2–1. Although not officially completed until 1937, the ground received national football stadium status in the early 1920s. In April 1937, a friendly international between Scotland and England had an official attendance of 149,515, a European record for an international, unlikely to be bettered in this age of all-seated stadiums. Scotland won 3–1.

Still remembered around the world as the greatest game ever is the European Cup final between Real Madrid and Eintracht Frankfurt at Hampden in 1960, when Real Madrid defeated Eintracht Frankfurt 7–3 to be crowned Europe's greatest side for the fifth consecutive season

By the late 1970s Hampden was crumbling, and in the 1980s the government went back on a promise to help refurbish it. In 1993 however, a redevelopment programme began, and in 1999 a new state-of-the-art stadium, with a sports injury fitness centre and the world's first national football museum, was unveiled.

Unfortunately, while Scotland has gained a magnificent new stadium, as its capacity is now only 52,000 instead of the previous six-figure crowds, it has lost the famous Hampden roar so intimidating to foreign teams.

In front of the stadium is Lesser Hampden where Queen's Park occasionally play. In front of it is Mount Florida Parish Church.

Hampden Park in 1927 with spectators streaming to the gates to get entry into an already chock-full stadium. Looking at this photograph it is hard to believe just how many people could be crowded into one space without there being a disaster. The view was taken before an international match but it is not known which one.
Courtesy of the Scottish Football Museum

1. Somerville Drive
2. Hampden Park
3. Lesser Hampden
4. Mount Florida
   Parish Church

1. Stables
2. Walled Garden
3. King's Park
4. Aitkenhead House
5. State Cinema
6. Castlemilk Crescent
7. Kingsbridge Drive
8. King's Park Primary School

King's Park 1950

Lying between Mount Florida and Cathcart on the west and Rutherglen to the east, King's Park developed between the wars as a commuter suburb built on the estate of Aitkenhead, bought by house builders Mactaggart and Mickel. To the north, the houses were built over the Hundred Acre Hill and Dyke, hence King's Acre Road and King's Dyke Avenue. In 1928, during construction of the houses there were two fatalities. One of them, a sixteen-year-old slater's apprentice, fell fifteen feet from scaffolding and died.

In the bottom left-hand quarter of the view is King's Park, gifted to the city in 1930 by Sir John Mactaggart. He also gifted Aitkenhead House (in the centre of the park), the country residence of West India merchant John Gordon, built in 1806, with wings added by David Hamilton in 1832. During the Second World War, it served as the Anti-Aircraft Headquarters of the Royal Artillery with a hutted encampment in the grounds. Developers divided it into flats in 1986, the first time that a building within a Glasgow park was adapted to private housing.

Bottom centre is the walled garden with, at its entrance, an ornate obelisk sundial made for the Earl of Hume that originally stood in the garden of Douglas Castle. It was re-erected in King's Park in 1958. Although the sundial was made in 1885 it is a copy of one constructed at Newbattle Abbey, Midlothian, in 1635.

King's Park Avenue runs full length across the middle of the view. The larger building at its right end is the Art Deco State Cinema, which closed in 1971. At its left end is the curving Kingsbridge Drive, with on its right the Art Deco King's Park Primary School, built on the site of Meikle-Aitkenhead Farm on the crest of Hundred Acre Hill. The children were evacuated at the beginning of the war but returned in 1941. Castlemilk Crescent is in the middle, between the cinema and the school.

Aitkenhead House, which was built on the site of a seventeenth-century house in 1806 with wings added in 1832. Its first owner was John Gordon, whose town house was on the east side of Buchanan Street on the site now occupied by the Prince of Wales Buildings, which incorporate Princes Square Shopping Mall. The Gordon family owned Aitkenhead until it was sold to Sir John Mactaggart in 1929. It is now divided into fourteen flats.

Carmunnock 1991

With the exception of the women hanging out the washing, this late nineteenth-century view of Carmunnock looks very similar today.

This view shows Carmunnock, Glasgow's only village that, despite being only six miles from the city centre and being very close to the ever-expanding East Kilbride, still preserves its identity and rural atmosphere. Anyone who lived there in the eighteenth century would still find it recognisable. No one knows from how early the community of Carmunnock existed, but signs of Bronze and Iron Age settlers have been found in the district.

The name Carmunnock is thought to derive either from the Gaelic *caer mynock* ('the monks' fort') or *caer bannauc* ('the hill fort'). Long ago, the spelling was Cormanoc. The patron saint of Carmunnock is St Cadoc, who founded a church here in ad 528. Prior to that, druids served the religious needs of the people.

This view shows the Carmunnock Conservation Area. Running diagonally across the view is Kirk Road, centre left of which is Carmunnock Parish Church, erected by order of the Presbytery of Glasgow in 1767 and built on the site of an earlier church. Its style is very much that of a typical eighteenth-century Scottish Reform Church.

At the church gates is the Watch House, built in the early nineteenth century to house guards who kept watch over the graves in the churchyard (which predates the church) during the 'Resurrectionist' era. The oldest tombstone is dated 1744. Alongside the churchyard are eighteenth-century dwellings.

East of the church, in Manse Road, is a row of restored eighteenth-century cottages. On the outside wall of No. 11 is an inset stone with the words 'the Schoolhouse 1702', indicating that the building once housed Carmunnock's first parish school. Manse Road was originally School Loan.

North of the schoolhouse is Clason Hall (the parish church hall) of 1865, the former Free Church Mission Hall. At the start of the twentieth century, the fortunes of the mission declined, and by 1918 services had discontinued. The hall then lay empty until the United Free Church Presbytery offered it to Carmunnock Kirk Session on a lease of £5 a year. The hall re-opened in 1924 and has been in use ever since.

Beyond Clason Hall is the former Boghead Inn, now an Indian restaurant. The building, thought to date from 1755, was originally Boghead Farm, which became the Boghead Inn in the late nineteenth or early twentieth century. The inn closed in 1974.

Left of the Boghead Inn is Castlemilk Hall (1893), built for the village on land purchased by William Stirling Stuart, Laird of Castlemilk. In October 1893, a grand party was held to open the hall, the Laird having instructed that each household had to receive an elegantly printed invitation to the event.

1. Eighteenth-century
   Dwellings
2. Churchyard
3. Carmunnock Parish
   Church
4. Eighteenth-century
   Dwellings
5. Castlemilk Hall
6. Former Boghead Inn
7. Clason Hall
8. The Schoolhouse

1. Old Cathcart Bridge
2. The Old Snuff Mill
3. 19th-century cottages
   and Lindsay House
4. The Old Smiddy
5. Old Cathcart Parish
   Church Belfry Tower
6. Cathcart Old Parish Church

Cathcart 1991

Crown copyright RCAHMS Ref. B71193CN

The name Cathcart is thought to derive from the Celtic caer, meaning 'fort', and cart, meaning 'stream'. Cathcart, a small village on the banks of the White Cart river, was one of three ancient parishes that ringed Glasgow to the south, the others being Govan and Eastwood. Its history goes back to the reign of King David I of Scotland (1124–53).

In 1791, with a population of only 697, the village was mainly agricultural, the only established industry being a paper mill at Millholm. By the early nineteenth century, the pure waters of the White Cart had attracted industries, and another village (New Cathcart) grew along the line of the road to Ayrshire, the present Clarkston Road. Grain mills, paper mills, dye and carpet works and an iron foundry lined the riverbanks, and by 1891 the population was 16,598.

When the railway reached Cathcart in 1886, wealthy city workers built fine villas between the old and new villages. Two decades later, Cathcart was a popular residential suburb that remained independent of Glasgow until 1912.

This view shows the old village. Extreme bottom left is Cathcart Old Bridge, believed to be late eighteenth century but confusingly bearing a datestone of 1624. It was once the only bridge crossing the river and important because it was on the main road from Glasgow to Ayr.

In front of the bridge is the Old Snuff Mill, built as a meal mill in the eighteenth century and converted into a paper mill producing cardboard in 1812. Two years later the small west section became a snuff mill. The remains of the mill and the Mill House of 1902 have been converted into housing. Right of the Snuff Mill are late nineteenth-century cottages and the tall, narrow crow-stepped Lindsay House of 1863.

Near the centre of the view is one of the oldest buildings in Cathcart, the Old Smiddy, which once housed the village blacksmith and a dog infirmary and is now a pub and restaurant.

Directly north of the Old Smiddy is a square belfry tower attached to a gable, all that remains of the Old Cathcart Parish Church of 1831. In the graveyard, which predates the church, is the grave of the Polmadie Martyrs: Robert Thome, Thomas Cook and John Urie, executed in 1685 for adhering to the Covenant. Right of the tower is Cathcart Old Parish Church, built to replace the 1831 church and opened in 1929.

Old Cathcart Bridge, painted by William Simpson around 1845, shows the two-arched bridge that resembles the Brig o' Doon. At the time of the painting, the area was one of great natural beauty. The chimney belongs to the mill now called the Old Snuff Mill. To the left is the watering hole originally known as the 'Wee Thack Hoose in the Glen' and later as Granny Robertson's Inn. Villas now take its place.

Queen's Park 1960

Camphill Art Gallery and Museum in Edwardian times. The compact four-square classical house has similarities to Aitkenhead House and, like it, has been attributed to David Hamilton, one of the city's most celebrated architects The view shows the front of the house with its portico of coupled Ionic columns. While at first an art gallery and museum, the building later became the Museum of Costume, which also housed a local exhibition that included items recovered from Langside battlefield.

Crown copyright P.543/RAF/996 0171

Glasgow has more parkland per square mile than any other city in the world and the south side has much of it. This view looks east over Queen's Park from Pollokshaws Road. Sir Joseph Paxton, the designer of the Crystal Palace, submitted plans for the park in 1860 that were mostly carried out except for a huge glass winter garden and a lake. Created on the land of Pathhead Farm, bought by the Corporation in 1857, the park opened in 1862. Owing to its situation, it escaped the bulk of the city's smoke, and in 1886 the Quiz periodical called it 'that most bracing of the lungs of the city'.

The building extreme bottom right in the view is Langside Halls, designed by John Gibson in 1847 and originally the premises of the National Bank of Scotland in Queen Street. When it was scheduled for demolition in 1901, the Corporation moved the Palladian-style building stone by stone to its present site and converted it into public halls in 1903. Royal arms flanked by the figures of Peace and Plenty grace the top of the building, and at ground-floor level bearded sculptured heads over the windows represent the rivers Clyde, Thames, Severn, Tweed and Humber.

Left of Langside Halls are bowling greens, now five-a-side football pitches with, to their left, Camphill House, which, along with its grounds, was added to the park in 1894. The house, built in the early nineteenth century, became an art gallery and museum in 1896 and is now converted into flats.

Left of the house in the view is the boating pond, which, along with its smaller neighbour was excavated out of the lawn of Camphill House in 1905. The area behind the pond was once a marsh called the 'Deil's Kirkyard'. Legend has it that the Catholic dead from the Battle of Langside were buried there as they were denied burial in Cathcart's Protestant churchyard. Bodies have never been found. North of the pond is the bandstand of the 1920s, which replaced the original, now in Motherwell's Duchess Park.

Centre right in the view is an earthwork of a circular camp measuring 330 by 390 feet. The once marshy area would have been a superb defensive position for a settlement or military camp, hence the name Camphill. Left of the earthwork, from which Roman and medieval remains have been uncovered, is the summit of Camphill, raised higher with an artificial mound from which the view over the city is magnificent.

Middle top is Third Lanark's Cathkin Park, originally the second Hampden Park.

1. Langside Public Halls
2. Camphill House
3. Pollokshaws Road
4. Boating Pond
5. Camphill Queen's
   Park Church
6. Bandstand
7. Earthwork
8. Camphill Summit
9. Cathkin Park

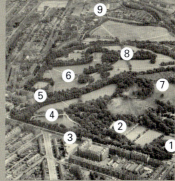

1. Langside Hill Church
2. Battle Place
   and Monument
3. Queen's Park
4. Victoria Infirmary
5. Langside College of
   Further Education
6. Former Deaf and
   Dumb Institution
7. Hampden Park
8. Cathkin Park

Langside 1991

In the middle of the nineteenth century Langside village was described as being a 'little hamlet finely situated near the ridge of a long hill which lies a little distance to the south west of Glasgow'. The long hill, now incorporated into Battlefield Road, gave rise to the name Langside, which then had about twenty single-storeyed cottages facing each other across a single street (now Algie Street). Inhabiting the cottages were mainly weavers, who in their spare time culti-vated apples and gooseberries for sale. Despite remain-ing unscathed when villas appeared in the 1850s, the village was swept away at the end of the century for tenement building, which continued as far south as the edge of the River Cart to form the new suburb of Battlefield.

Within the circle near the centre of the view (the site of the original village) is Battle Place, scene of the Battle of Langside on 13 May 1568 between the forces of Mary Queen of Scots and those of her half-brother, Regent Moray. Although Mary had six thousand men and Moray four thousand, within forty-five minutes Mary's troops had been defeated. Mary, supposed to have watched the battle from Cathcart Hill, fled towards England. In the centre of Battle Place is Langside Monument, erected in 1887 to commemo-rate the battle. Previously there was a row of thatched cottages known as the 'Cruikit Raw'.

In front of Battle Place is the Graeco-Roman style Langside Hill Church of 1895, designed by local archi-tect Alexander Skirving. The church, built for the Free Church of Scotland, was the last classical church built in Glasgow. After standing almost in ruins for several years it was restored and reopened as the Church on the Hill bar and restaurant.

Centre in the view is the Victoria Infirmary, the 'Vicky' to southsiders. Building began in 1888, and the main entrance facing Queen's Park has a central pedi-mented gable flanked by rooftop towers. On the gable are the arms of Queen Victoria with, above them, the figure of a puma, the symbol of medical care. The

Designed by Alexander Skirving, the memorial commemorating the Battle of Langside was erected in 1887 on the 300th anniversary of Queen Mary's death. The lion at the top of the 58-foot-high monument rests his paw on a cannon ball and faces Clincart Hill (where the former Deaf and Dumb Institution now is) and where Mary's forces were positioned. *Courtesy of Glasgow Development and Regeneration Services*

hospital had an innovative ventilation system that could completely change its air in eight minutes. This was to ensure that 'none of the inmates will ever breathe air which had previously passed through the lungs of any of the other occupants'.

The modern buildings right of the Infirmary belong to Langside College of Further Education. Left of the college is the former Deaf and Dumb Institution of 1876, which became part of the college in 1947 but has now been converted to housing. Left in the view is Queen's Park. Top centre is Hampden Park.

Pollok House and Gardens 2006

This view shows Pollok House and its gardens, part of Pollok Estate, which came into the hands of the Maxwell family in the mid-thirteenth century where it remained until Mrs Anne Maxwell Macdonald gifted Pollok House and its grounds to the city in 1966. Since 1911, 121 acres of the estate had been open to the public as a park.

Pollok House, centre left in the view with the White Cart river in front of it, is attributed to William Adam and believed to be the fourth Maxwell dwelling on the site, the first three being castles. Completed in 1752, the well-proportioned four-storey house is almost austere. Wings and a terrace designed by Robert Rowand Anderson were added between 1890 and 1908. As they spoiled the view from the house, the homes of the estate workers were demolished and the families rehoused in nearby Shawlands.

Sir John Stirling Maxwell (1866–1956) largely created the gardens and began by planting the lime avenue leading to the north front of the house. Consisting mainly of trees and shrubs such as magnolias and azaleas, the gardens are of great horticultural value. As rhododendrons were of particular interest to Sir John, they feature extensively. Sir John was one of the founders of the National Trust for Scotland, which, since 1998, has managed Pollok House on behalf of the city.

The quadrangle in the view is the late eighteenth-century Old Stable Courtyard built on the site of the Laigh Castle, the third Maxwell castle. Incorporated into the courtyard are relics of a tower added to the castle in 1536. In front of the courtyard is the Countryside Rangers' Centre, originally a small chapel. Alongside are the mid-nineteenth-century sawmill and the early twentieth-century power station and the battery house, which once supplied power to the estate and the 'big house'. The mill weir still crosses the river.

Behind the stable courtyard is the Demonstration Garden with flowers, fruit, vegetables, shrubs and trees arranged so that gardeners can get inspiration for their own gardens. There are also formal gardens, a rose garden to sit in and greenhouses to walk through. Behind is the Woodland Garden with, at its highest point, an enormous beech tree that marks the site of the second Pollok castle. In the foreground is Pollok Golf Course.

A view of the south side of Pollok House showing the wings and terrace added by Robert Rowand Anderson. The house is open to the public and has one of the finest collections of Spanish paintings in the country, including works by El Greco, Goya and Murillo. The furniture is mainly Chippendale and Sheraton.

1. Pollok Golf Course
2. White Cart Water
3. The Mill Weir
4. Sawmill, Power Station and Battery House
5. Countryside Rangers' Centre
6. Old Stable Courtyard
7. Demonstration Garden
8. Woodland Garden
9. Pollok House
10. Lime Avenue

1. Peace Cairn
2. Walled Garden
3. The House for an Art Lover
4. Glasgow Ski Centre
5. Palace of Art

Bellahouston Park 2005

The land forming Bellahouston Park was acquired in 1895, with the addition of part of the lands of Dumbreck in 1901 and the lands of Ibroxhill in 1903, purchased to provide a better entrance to the park and to preserve the well-wooded grounds. The park centres on a 170-foot-high wooded hill with level ground surrounding it on three sides.

The most important event in the park's history was when it hosted the 1938 Empire Exhibition. Kelvingrove, the venue for the previous major exhibitions, lacked sufficient level ground to accommodate the enormous size of the event, which was to cover at least twice the area of the earlier exhibitions. As the exhibition took place just after the Depression and when war threatened, the city badly needed the boost such an event could bring in promoting industry and raising morale.

The exhibition's architect was Thomas Smith Tait, who planned three main avenues on the flat land but said the hill would be sacrosanct and would have a tower on top of it, nothing else. Although grandly named the Tower of Empire, it quickly became Tait's Tower. As the hill was 170 feet high and the tower 330 feet high, it was visible 100 miles away. It was meant to be a permanent structure but was demolished in 1939, as it would have been a navigational aid for enemy warplanes.

The largest pavilions were the Palaces of Engineering and Industry with exhibits from the empire's dominions and colonies. A long narrow pond with cascading fountains separated the buildings.

There are only three reminders of the exhibition left in the park, one the granite Exhibition Memorial unveiled in 1937 by King George VI. The others are the Palace of Art and the Peace Cairn, erected in 1938 as a lasting reminder of people's hopes and fears. The cairn has stone blocks engraved with the names of organisations that were deeply concerned with the possibility of war. The Palace of Art is top right in the view, the Peace Cairn bottom left.

Near the centre is the House for an Art Lover (1989–96), built on the foundations of Ibroxhill House to a 1901 design by Charles Rennie Mackintosh. As Mackintosh's plans were incomplete, however, imagination has gone into the building's final design. Since it opened to the public, the house has developed a reputation as one of Glasgow's premier cultural attractions, welcoming over 100,000 overseas visitors each year. Left of the house are the Walled Gardens, the kitchen garden of Ibroxhill House. North of the Gardens is the outdoor Glasgow Ski Centre, which replaced the bandstand.

In 1982 the park became an open-air cathedral when Pope John Paul II held a mass there when he visited Glasgow.

This postcard of the 1938 Empire Exhibition shows the Palace of Art at the foot of the Scottish Avenue.

SCOTTISH AVENUE, EMPIRE EXHIBITION, SCOTLAND 1938   X67

Glasgow International Airport 2005

This view shows Glasgow International Airport, with the White Cart River in the foreground and the M8 motorway on the left.

While the airport opened for commercial traffic on 2 May 1966, its origin goes back to 1932 when it was developed at Abbotsinch to accommodate the 602 (City of Glasgow) Squadron of the Auxiliary Air Force, which was short of space at nearby Renfrew aerodrome. The Squadron moved in on 20 January 1933 and remained there until the start of the Second World War when it was mobilised for full time RAF duty and transferred to the east of Scotland to protect the naval base at Rosyth and coastal shipping. The 602 was the first auxiliary squadron to be equipped with the new super-fighter, the Supermarine Spitfire. This was ahead of many of the regular RAF squadrons.

Prior to the 602 moving out, other RAF units had used the airfield, but in 1943 control of it passed to the Royal Navy, and HMS *Sanderling*, as it was called, was commissioned on 20 September.

Both Renfrew and Abbotsinch played an important role during the war. Being convenient to both the docks and the Clyde estuary, they were ideal as aircraft receiving and maintenance bases. The Fleet Air Arm used Abbotsinch as an aircraft maintenance yard and training station.

After the war, Renfrew resumed service as Glasgow's civil airport while Abbotsinch served as a repair base for British, American and Canadian fighter aircraft as well as being used as a dump for old aircraft.

Although HMS *Sanderling* closed in 1963, the airfield's future was secured as in 1964 the city announced that Abbotsinch would be developed as the new Glasgow Airport, Renfrew having reached its limit of expansion. The first terminal building was designed by Sir Basil Spence's practice.

Although the first scheduled flight to land officially at the new Abbotsinch Airport on 2 May 1966, was BEA Herald G-APWB carrying forty-one passengers from Aberdeen and Edinburgh, five days before an RAF Pembroke landed, the pilot having mistaken the runway for that of Renfrew's.

Probably the busiest day ever at the airport was on 12 May 1976 when the European Cup final between Bayern Munich and St Etienne was played at Hampden. Sixty-four assorted aircraft had landed at the airfield by kick-off.

In 1975 the city handed the airport over to the British Airports Authority. By 1986 it was the fourth busiest airport in Britain and became even busier when transatlantic flights began in 1990.

Glasgow Airport, Scotland's busiest with almost nine million passengers a year flying to over 100 destinations worldwide, celebrated its fortieth birthday on 2 May 2006.

This view of 1946 of the same area as that opposite shows a very different Abbotsinch Airport. Here the aircraft hangars wear their wartime camouflage, and the rows of small uniform buildings to the left are Nissen huts. The planes here are waiting to be scrapped, one of the uses of the airfield after the war. There is also no M8 motorway, although it is easy to see where it was constructed.

Crown copyright RCAHMS 106G/UK 1383 6057

1. White Cart Water
2. M8 Motorway
3. Terminal Building
4. Control Tower
5. Runways

1. Edmiston Drive
2. Main Stand

Ibrox Park 2005

This view shows Ibrox Park, the stadium of Rangers Football Club, founded in 1873 by a group of men who played football on Fleshers' Haugh in Glasgow Green. Ibrox was not the site of the club's first ground, which was at Burnbank, off Great Western Road. Then came Kinning Park, and in 1887 the first Ibrox, where, on 7 November 1891, Buffalo Bill watched Rangers play Queen's Park. Rangers lost 3–0. In 1899, when the landlord wanted back part of their ground, Rangers made another move, the shortest in football history as the new site offered was only 100 yards away.

To raise the money to build a stadium the club went public, raising £12,000. Archibald Leitch, a famous football ground architect, designed the stadium, a timber-lattice structure with sweeping, high-backed terracings supported by scaffolding comprising large beams of timber criss-crossing each other. At the time, the average attendance at a game was 15,000, rising to around 40,000 for games against Celtic. In 1902, however, when Ibrox was chosen as the venue for a Scotland versus England international, a crowd of 70,000 was anticipated. When even more attended, part of the west terracing collapsed, throwing hundreds of spectators to the ground. Twenty-five died and over 500 were injured. The disaster led to the end of wooden terracings and the introduction of earth banks.

After purchasing its ground in 1904, Rangers started improvements, including an athletics track where Olympian Eric Liddell trained. The Main Stand, facing Edmiston Drive in the view, designed by Archibald Leitch and now a listed building, opened in 1929 with seating for 10,500 people. In 1936 a Nazi swastika flew over Ibrox Park, the reason for its presence being that the Scottish Football Association had invited the German international team to play Scotland at Ibrox Park and, as custom dictated, the flag of the visiting country was prominently displayed on the roof of the main grandstand.

There was a second disaster at Ibrox on 2 January 1971 when over 80,000 supporters watched the traditional New Year derby between Rangers and Celtic. The game was exciting, with Jimmy Johnstone scoring for Celtic in the 89th minute and Colin Stein equalising for Rangers in injury time. Disaster then unfolded at Staircase 13. A terrifying crush engulfed supporters, and barriers and handrails were bent and twisted. Sixty-six fans died and 145 were injured.

The disaster resulted in the transformation of Ibrox into one of Europe's most envied football stadiums, with four stands and a seating capacity of around 50,000, substantially less than the record attendance of 1939 when Rangers played Celtic in front of 118,567 people.

The main stand at Ibrox Park in the 1920s. Note just how many women there are in the seated part.

Govan Cross 2005

The Pearce Institute designed by Robert Rowand Anderson in seventeenth-century Scottish Renaissance style and endowed by Lady Pearce in memory of her husband, Sir William Pearce, who, along with the Elders and Napiers, did much to make the Clyde the greatest shipbuilding river in the world. Beneath the foundations of the institute lie what is thought to be the ancient holy well of St Constantine. Across the street from the institute is a statue of Sir William, known locally as the 'Black Man' because of the bronze being discoloured and tarnished by the elements.
Crown copyright RCAHMS Ref. C/070044

While Govan can trace its ecclesiastical history to the sixth century, the first written reference is in a charter of 1136 granting its lands and church to the see of Glasgow. A village developed around the important religious site now occupied by Govan Old Parish Church, and by the sixteenth century Bishop Leslie was describing Govan as 'a gret and large village upon the water of Clyd named Govan whare ale is wondrous guid'.

The Govan of today is only a fragment of the original parish that once stretched to Gorbals and Govanhill in the east, Strathbungo and Dumbreck in the south and Kelvinside in the north. During the eighteenth century, villagers lived by salmon fishing and weaving. Change was on the way, however, and shipbuilding, begun by Macarthur Alexander in 1839 just east of the Cross, was to transform Govan.

This view shows what is left of old Govan Cross. Middle right is the former Govan Ferry landing stage leading to Water Row, once lined by picturesque thatched cottages. Bottom right is the church of 1873 known as St Mary's until 1982 when it united with other congregations and became Govan New Church. Left of the church is the former British Linen Bank building of 1900 topped with an open crown. Opposite the bank is the shopping centre and bus station.

Left of the bank is the Pearce Institute, endowed to the people of Govan in 1906 by Lady Pearce. On the door are the words: 'This is a house of friendship. This is a house of service. For families. For lonely folk. For the people of Govan. For the strangers of the world. Welcome.' Among facilities were reading rooms, a library, gymnasium, and cooking and laundry departments. After being closed for a couple of years for structural repairs, the institute is bustling again.

Adjacent to the institute, set back in its graveyard, is Old Govan Church, designed by Robert Rowand Anderson and opened in 1888. The site is more interesting than the church, as tradition has it that in the middle of the sixth century St Constantine, who came from Cornwall, founded a monastery on or near it.

Inside the church is possibly Scotland's richest collection of early Christian sculptures. The most amazing is the Govan Sarcophagus, a shrine coffin with a hole in the base that allowed the decomposing matter from the body to drain out of the coffin. Among the other sculptures is the shaft of the Celtic Govan Cross, the Sun Stone, possibly pagan, and five hogback burial stones that suggest tenth-century Viking settlement. The graveyard is the only part of pre-industrial Govan to survive and contains seventeenth-, eighteenth- and nineteenth-century gravestones.

1. Old Govan Ferry
   Landing Stage
2. Govan New Church
3. Govan Cross
4. Former British Linen Bank
5. Shopping Centre
6. Pearce Institute
7. Govan Old Parish
   Church and Graveyard
8. St Anthony's Catholic Church

The East End

Tollcross Park

Tollcross Park in the autumn of 2005. At the end of the
nineteenth century the industrial east end of the city had
no central open space for recreation. Difficulty was had
in securing a site for a park until Tollcross Estate was
purchased in 1896 from James Dunlop, a proprietor of
the Clyde Ironworks. The estate, which included the
Baronial-style Tollcross House, centre right in the view,
was converted into Tollcross Park and opened in 1897.
Top right are the Winter Gardens and conservatories.
Flowerbeds are laid out in Rennie Mackintosh patterns.
Crown copyright RCAHMS Ref. DP9898

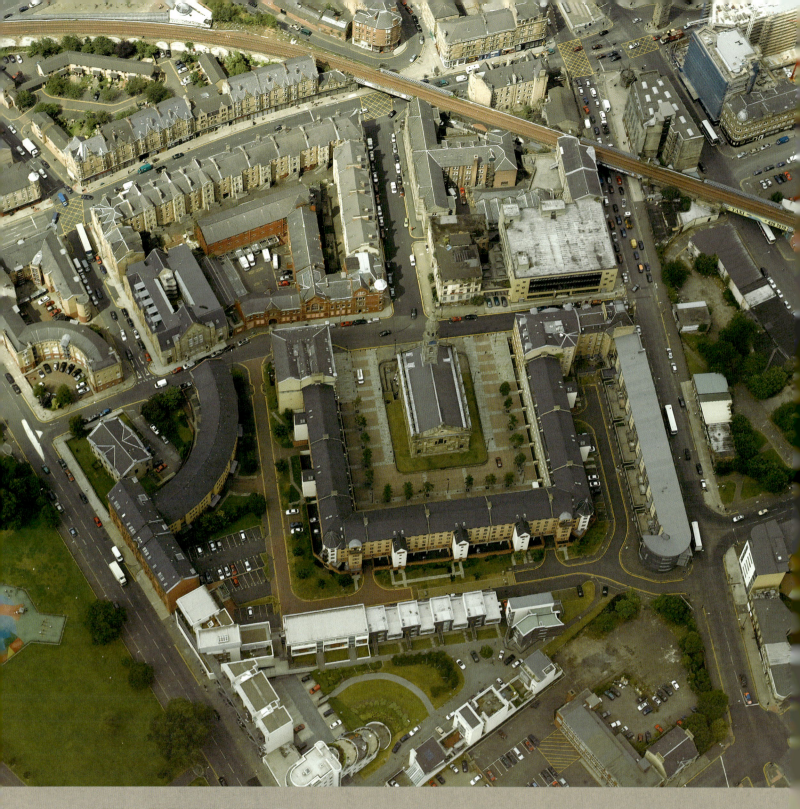

1. Tolbooth Steeple
2. Saltmarket
3. City of Glasgow Union Railway Viaduct
4. Gallowgate
5. London Road
6. St Andrew's Parish Church
7. St Andrew's Square
8. St Andrew's-by-the-Green Church
9. Greendyke Street
10. Glasgow Green
11. Eighteenth-century house, Charlotte Street
12. Homes for the twenty-first century

St Andrew's Square 2005

Crown copyright RCAHMS Ref. DP9926

The railway viaduct running diagonally across the top of this photograph effectively forms the eastern boundary of the city centre. The transition between the city centre and the east end is abrupt. Within a short distance, the large stores and commercial premises of Argyle Street give way to tenements and small shops in Gallowgate and London Road. It was not always like that, however. In the eighteenth century the aristocracy favoured the area in the view, St Andrew's Square, built around St Andrew's Parish Church, the first post-Reformation church built in Glasgow.

The church of 1739–56, modelled, except for the tower, by architect Allan Dreghorn and mason Mungo Naismith on St Martin's-in-the-Fields in London, predates the square. Its giant portico of six Corinthian columns supports a pediment bearing Glasgow's coat of arms. Above that is a clock tower with an octagonal bell chamber. The stone to build the church came from the Crackling House Quarry, where Queen Street Station now stands. In 1785 the Italian balloonist Vincenzo Lunardi made two flights from the back of the church, which today is A-listed inside and outside and is now the Centre for Scottish Music and Dance.

Planned in 1786, St Andrew's Square consisted of three-storey classical houses distinguished by fanlights and pediments. By 1802, commercial premises had crept in and eventually dominated the square. Nothing remains of the original housing, but buildings such as the Italianate leather warehouse of 1876 on the south-west corner have been converted to housing. New residential buildings have filled in gaps around the square.

From right to left the principal vertical thoroughfares are Gallowgate, London Road and Greendyke Street. Saltmarket runs across the top, with the Tolbooth Steeple to the right at Glasgow Cross. Turnbull Street runs behind the square.

Beside Glasgow Green, bottom left, is the former St Andrew's-by-the-Green Church (1750), the oldest surviving Episcopal church building in Scotland. The

St Andrew's Parish Church, the most impressive eighteenth-century church in Scotland. Its massive portico caused such alarm that it is said that the night before the props were to be removed its stonemason, Mungo Naismith, spent the night beneath it to demonstrate its safety. Allan Dreghorn, its architect, was a wealthy coachbuilder and timber merchant. The interior of the church is magnificent, the carved woodwork coming from Dreghorn's workshops. In the same year that Naismith finished work on St Andrew's, Glasgow Cathedral's spire was hit by lightning and condemned. Naismith came to the rescue and saved it by his reconstruction.
Courtesy of Glasgow Development and Regeneration Services

Episcopalians were unpopular in Glasgow and were known as 'piskies'. The church was built primarily as a chapel for the English soldiers stationed in an infantry barracks near what is now Barracks Street. As it was the first church in Scotland to use an organ in its services, it was nicknamed the 'Whistling Kirk'. After years of being threatened by removal, the church was converted into offices.

Glasgow Green 1930

Originally, Glasgow Green was not where it is at present. Known as the Dovecote Green (later the Old Green), it extended from the Clyde to Argyle Street and from Stockwell Street to Jamaica Street. Around 1700 it was a fashionable promenade shaded by trees, but eventually the town encroached on it until it disappeared.

The present green was once part of the Bishop's Forest, east of the city. It is unknown when it became the property of the community, but in 1450 James II made a grant of land to Bishop Turnbull who supposedly presented it to the community.

In the sixteenth century the common lands were sold, except for the Low Green, approximately between today's High Court and the Nelson Monument and the Clyde and Monteith Row. From 1662 until 1792, the town re-acquired land east of the Low Green – the High Green, Calton Green, King's Park and Fleshers' Haugh. An area between Saltmarket and Stockwell where slaughterhouses, tan pits and glue works proliferated became Skinners' Green.

Although laid out with serpentine walks and shrubberies, the 'New Green' was used for communal purposes – washing and bleaching linen, grazing of the town's livestock, and for playing golf and other games. Both Rangers (1873) and Celtic (1888) Football Clubs originated there. The layout of the Green we know today was begun around 1813.

As the photograph shows, the course of the Clyde governs the contour of the Green's southern boundary. The triangular shape at the bottom of the view is roughly the area of the old Low Green. The High Green reached to King's Drive, which curves on to King's Bridge, leading to Hutchesontown. Beyond King's Drive to the left is King's Park and to the right Fleshers' Haugh, so named as the early fleshing trade was there. Bonnie Prince Charlie reviewed his troops there when he made his unwelcome visit to Glasgow in December 1745. Calton Green has been built over.

In the centre of the triangle is the Doulton Fountain by A. E. Pearse, the principal exhibit at the Glasgow International Exhibition of 1888 in Kelvingrove Park and re-erected on the Green in 1890. Beyond the fountain is the Nelson Monument (1806), the first in Britain erected to commemorate Lord Nelson's victories. The area around the monument was the city's first golf course.

Left of the monument is the People's Palace (1893), built as a cultural centre for the deprived east-enders and comprising a museum, picture gallery and music hall. Adjoining the palace are the Winter Gardens the glazed roof of which supposedly represents the inverted hull of Lord Nelson's flagship, *Victory*. Beyond the palace is the multi-coloured Templeton's carpet factory, designed by William Leiper in 1889 and modelled on Venice's Doge's Palace.

Simmons Aerofilms

This view of 2006 shows the People's Palace, the Winter Gardens, the Doulton Fountain and the former Templeton carpet factory. Where it differs from the 1930 view is that the largest terracotta fountain in the world, gifted to the city by Sir Henry Doulton, is now in front of the People's Palace. It was re-sited there after restoration, and on 9 May 2005 was switched on for the first time in forty years. Another change from 1930 is that Templeton's factory, now converted into offices and houses, has extended round to London Road. There was a terrible tragedy during the construction of this architectural gem of a factory. On 1 November 1889, a partially built wall collapsed through the roof of the adjoining weaving shed, killing twenty-nine women and injuring twenty.
Crown copyright RCAHMS Ref. DP9919

1. Doulton Fountain
2. Nelson Monument
3. People's Palace
   and Winter Gardens
4. Templeton's Carpet Factory
5. Bridgeton
6. Dalmarnock
7. King's Park
8. Fleshers' Haugh
9. King's Bridge
10. Hutchesontown

1. Orr Street
2. Broad Street
3. Olympia Street
4. London Road
5. Bridgeton Cross
6. Dalmarnock Road
7. Main Street
8. James Street
9. Bridgeton Central Station
10. Templeton Carpet Factory

Bridgeton 1979

Bridgeton Cross with its famous 'Umbrella' in the centre. Erected to shelter the unemployed during the depression of the 1870s and donated by the Sun Foundry, its bright red roof is topped by a square clock tower and fancy weathervane. The building to the right of the shelter started life in 1911 as the Olympia Theatre of Varieties. It then became the Olympia Cinema and after that a bingo hall. It is now unoccupied. John Turnbull designed the red-sandstone tenements left of the theatre in 1897.

Vertical aerial photographs provide a very clear view of street layouts. This one of Bridgeton shows its streets radiating out from Bridgeton Cross.

Bridgeton was known as Barrowfield until Rutherglen Bridge was built at its southern end in 1776 and a new road was constructed from there to the village's north boundary at what is now known as Bridgeton Cross. Within two years the new road had become Main Street, Bridgetown, and then Bridgeton.

Bridgeton was an early industrial centre of Glasgow. As far back as 1785, George MacIntosh and David Dale set up the Barrowfield Dyeworks, the first Turkey red dyeing works in Britain. Associated trades such as cotton mills and bleachworks were introduced, and to house the workforce new streets appeared named after reformers such as Dale, Howard and Franklin. Papillon Street (now French Street) was named after Frenchman Pierre Papillon who advised George MacIntosh on the new dyeing process.

Before industrialisation Bridgeton was a weaving village. During a riot in 1787, opposing a wage reduction, three weavers were killed and several injured. Those killed were buried in Abercrombie Street graveyard where a memorial stone gives a brief history of their fate.

Bridgeton Cross is the small triangular area near the centre of the view. It stands at a seven-way junction that the City Improvement Trust formed in the 1870s, the Cross originally being at the intersection of Reid and Dale Streets. In the centre of the Cross is the famous East End landmark the 'Umbrella', an octagonal cast-iron shelter. Superior tenements, such as Bridgeton Cross Mansions (1899), surround the Cross, which is virtually unchanged since 1911.

Vertically centre in the view is Main Street, once filled with mills, factories and tenement housing. Today there is modern housing, landscaping and gap sites. Many of the street names off Main Street recall Bridgeton's textile past – Muslin, Poplin, Mill and Madras. The curved street to the right of Main Street is Dalmarnock Road, leading to Rutherglen. Left of Main Street is James Street, built on the lands of the old Bridgeton Green used for washing, bleaching and drying clothes. James Street, leading to Glasgow Green, was where Singer first manufactured their sewing machines before moving to Clydebank in 1884.

Top left in the view, curving to the right, is London Road, once Canning Street, named after the nineteenth-century prime minister, George Canning. Top left, facing London Road, is the former Templeton carpet factory. North of the Cross is Orr Street, named after John Orr who once owned Barrowfield estate. Olympia Street is the short street to the right of Orr Street. North from Olympia Street is Broad Street.

Dalmarnock 1960

Dalmarnock Power Station and Dalmarnock Bridge in the 1930s. The No. 26 tramcar plied between Scotstoun and Burnside. The tenement to the right, plastered with advertisements for McEwan's Beer and Cadbury's Drinking Chocolate, is one of the few remaining in the district. Modern housing has replaced the rest.

Although unattractive, this view of Dalmarnock records some of the industry that once dominated the area. As early business ventures depended on water for power, Dalmarnock was appealing because of its extensive river frontage and its nearness to Glasgow. In addition, it had large areas of undeveloped land.

Among Dalmarnock's industrial greats was, and is, Begg, Coulson & Co. Ltd in Springfield Road who manufactured special wire for Lord Kelvin when he conducted his experiments in electricity at Glasgow University. It also provided materials for Clyde-built ships, including the *Queen Mary*. The greatest firm however, was Sir William Arrol's Dalmarnock Works at Dunn Street, founded in 1868. It built such world-famous structures as the Forth Railway Bridge, London's Tower Bridge and the second Tay Bridge. It also built four Titan cranes for use on the River Clyde, all of which remain, with listed status.

For centuries Dalmarnock was strategically important because of its ford over the Clyde. Wooden bridges were built in 1821 and 1848, the latter surviving until the bridge near the centre in the view was opened in 1891. It was the first major bridge in Glasgow to have a completely flat surface. Upriver is the Caledonian Railway viaduct.

Left of the bridge in Rutherglen is Stewart & Lloyd's Phoenix Tube Works, which covered twelve acres and once employed 2,000 men. During the Second World War, after D-Day in June 1944, it helped lay pipes under the English Channel to supply the Allied forces with fuel. By 1950 the workforce was only 600, and eventually British Steel used the buildings as a warehouse. The site is now a wasteland. In front of the Tube Works are the San-Mex Chemical Works, still operating.

Because of its riverside location, Dalmarnock attracted service industries such as the power station right of the bridge. Begun by Glasgow Corporation Electricity Department in 1914, it occupied the site of Dalmarnock House. Note the coal stock yard at the rear. Although the site is derelict, there is a plan for it to become a 2014 Commonwealth Games venue. Right of the power station, stretching to the river, are works such as the Dalmarnock Weaving Factory, the Clyde Spinning Mills and Caledonian Ironworks.

At the river bend is Dalmarnock Sewage Works (1894), Glasgow's first sewage purification system and apparently so successful that the effluent discharged into the river was such that the works manager boasted of having kept a live goldfish in it in perfect health.

Top right is Shawfield Stadium, once the home of Clyde Football Club. To its right is Oatlands and Richmond Park.

1. San-Mex Chemical Works
2. Dalmarnock Bridge
3. Stewart & Lloyd's Tube Works
4. Caledonian Railway Viaducts
5. Dalmarnock Sewage Works
6. Shawfield Stadium
7. Dalmarnock Power Station

1. Parkhead Forge
   Shopping Centre
2. Gallowgate
3. Janefield Cemetery
   (Eastern Necropolis)
4. A. G. Barr's Factory
5. Celtic Park
6. London Road

Parkhead and Celtic Football Stadium 1998

Until the eighteenth century, Parkhead consisted of an inn and a few cottages at the 'Sheddens', later Parkhead Cross. By the 1820s it had grown into a small weaving village at the junction of two main routes, the Great Eastern Road (now Gallowgate) and Tollcross Road, and Westmuir Street. The status of the area changed to industrial with the opening of iron and chemical works along the Camlachie Burn. The major employer was Parkhead Forge, founded in 1837 by ironmaster John Reoch, who transformed scrap metal into forgings for all kinds of machinery, including steam engines for land and marine use. In 1841 Reoch sold the business to shipbuilder and engineer David Napier, who appointed William Rigby as manager. When Rigby died in 1863, William Beardmore took control of the business, which, until its closure in 1973, was always known as Beardmore's.

Top middle in the photograph is Parkhead Forge Shopping Centre, built over the massive Beardmore site. Diagonally in front of the Forge are the premises of A. G. Barr, the manufacturer of Scotland's other national drink, Irn-Bru, the drink 'made from girders'. Barr began manufacturing soft drinks in 1887 in the Gallowgate, the street running horizontally in front of the Forge. Always innovative in its advertising, for years Barr promoted Irn-Bru with a strip cartoon chronicling the adventures of Ba Bru, a turbaned Indian boy, and his pal Sandy, a kilted Scot. Production has now ceased at the Gallowgate site.

Dominating the view is Celtic Park, the home of Celtic Football Club, founded by the Irish Marist Brother Walfrid in Bridgeton to raise money for the district's poor children. The first Celtic Park was on the southwest of Janefield Cemetery (behind Celtic Park in the view) on the site now occupied by A. G. Barr. Celtic played its first game there on 28 May 1888, beating Rangers 5–2. When the club moved to its present site in 1892, it was described 'as having left a graveyard for Paradise', a name that has stuck since.

Few know that during the First World War a team of female munitions workers from Beardmore's Forge played at the Park, raising hundreds of pounds for charity and entertaining thousands with their skill. Women played at the Park until 1921 when the British Football Association banned the women's game. London Road runs diagonally across the front of Celtic Park.

The photograph opposite shows Celtic's magnificent new stadium, begun in the late 1990s. This photograph shows the old Celtic Park with its rows of terracing. *Crown copyright RCAHMS Ref. B55447CN*

Dennistoun 1950

Crown copyright RCAHMS PEFO 540/A/473 0285

This crowded view looks north over Dennistoun, named after Alexander Dennistoun who added to his Golfhill estate the neighbouring properties of Annfield, Broom Park, Whitehill, Craig Park, Wester Craigs, Meadow Park and Easter Craigs. Dennistoun asked architect James Salmon to have the areas laid out as an upper-class suburb of terraces and detached villas. What was done, however, was not to Salmon's plan. While the streets west of Whitehill had villas, from 1869 the rest were developed more lucratively with good-quality tenements for the middle classes. The east end of the city had not proved attractive to potential villa dwellers.

This lower half of the view shows the largely tenemented area between the Necropolis on the left and Craigpark Street on the right. Duke Street runs full length across the lower quarter of the view, and the Monkland Canal and Alexandra Parade run horizontally beyond the Necropolis. Beyond them is Royston.

Craigpark is the slanting street right in the view. The large square building at its north end is the former W. D & H. O. Wills' cigarette factory, started in 1946 and still under construction in 1950. Left of Craigpark is Westercraigs, with villas on its west side. Annfield Place, fronting Duke Street, runs horizontally between Craigpark and Westercraigs. After Westercraigs is Cardross Street, the curved building at its foot being Duke Street Hospital. Next is Dunchattan Street, then Ark Lane forking left into Firpark Street alongside the Necropolis. The mass bottom left is the abattoir, cattle and meat market, now demolished. At one time the cattle market was a great open-stalled space that stretched between Duke Street and Gallowgate where there was a weekly gathering of stock from all parts of the neighbouring country. The feeing market for servants was also there.

Top. The B-listed Annfield Place on the north side of Duke Street, two neat terraces of two-storey houses of 1851 named after Ann Park, the wife of James Tennant, who built Annfield Mansion.
Crown copyright RCAHMS Ref GW/3553

Above. W. D. & H. O. Wills' cigarette factory in 1984, now business premises. Note the famous names advertised – Capstan, Golden Virginia, Castella, and Will's Whiffs, all once produced in Dennistoun.
Crown copyright RCAHMS Ref. B25363

1. W. D. & H. O. Wills'
   Cigarette Factory
2. Craigpark Street
3. Annfield Place
4. Westercraigs
5. Duke Street
6. Cardross Street
7. Duke Street Hospital
8. Abattoir, Cattle and
   Meat Market
9. Dunchattan Street
10. Ark Lane
11. Firpark Street
12. Necropolis

Alexandra Park 2006

In 1866 the City Improvement Trust bought part of the estate of Haghill, known as Wester Kennyhill, to provide the northeastern district with a park and recreation ground. Recognising that the proximity of a public park would be beneficial in the development of his adjoining estate, Alexander Dennistoun gifted another five acres of land, providing a main entrance to the park in Alexandra Parade.

The work of laying out the park was carried out by 'unemployed starving artisans and labourers'. As the area was windswept, cold and polluted from nearby industry, however, it was difficult to cultivate. In 1891 the lands of Easter Kennyhill were added. Amenities included bowling greens, an open-air swimming pool formed from a disused freestone quarry, and an eighteen-hole golf course that in 1910 cost the modest sum of 3d a round. Near the flower gardens was a miniature lake with an adjoining model yacht pond.

This view of the park is bounded at the top by Provan Road with, to its left, the M8 motorway. Alexandra Parade is in the bottom right-hand corner, with, to its left, an avenue of trees, to the right of which, within the circular area, is the cast-iron MacFarlane Fountain, designed by the Saracen Foundry as a centrepiece for the Glasgow International Exhibition in 1901. North of the park is the golf course with tennis courts, football pitches, model yacht pond and miniature lake to the south.

Above Alexandra Parade, facing a bowling green, is Kennyhill Square, to the left of which is the Arts and Crafts-style St Andrew's East Church of 1903.
Crown copyright RCAHMS Ref. DP9928

The West End

Great Western Road and Kelvin Bridge

This view taken in 2006 shows Great Western Road and
Kelvin Bridge, which carries the road over the River Kelvin.
For some time after its opening in 1891, the bridge was
jokingly known as the 'tombstone bridge' because of the
four panels on each side bearing the names of the council-
lors forming the committee concerned with its construction.
The names were later removed. North of the bridge, set in
its grounds, is Glasgow Academy, designed by H. & D.
Barclay in 1878. To its left is Belmont Crescent. Right of
the bridge is Lansdowne Parish Church (1862–3), the most
striking of Glasgow's Gothic Revival churches. Left of the
bridge is the Scottish Arts and Crafts-style Caledonian
Mansions, designed by James Miller in 1895 for the
Caledonian Railway Company as an annexe to its Central
Hotel but never used as such. *Mitchell Library*

St George's Cross 1989

Crown copyright RCAHMS B21503CN

St George's Cross, Charing Cross and Anderston Cross have long marked the start of the West End. The Inner Ring Motorway, begun in the 1960s, which isolated the city centre from areas to the north, southwest and the fashionable West End cut through these once important road junctions.

The once grand St George's Road was a busy traffic and commercial area. Wood and Selby's Department Store occupied premises on both sides of the road, and the Empress Theatre, later Jimmy Logan's Metropole, was on the west side. St George's Cross, once a busy five-way junction, is now flanked by the carriageways of St George's Cross Interchange. Pierre Emile L'Angelier, the lover of Madeleine Smith, died in agony of arsenic poisoning in his lodgings near St George's Cross.

This photograph gives a superb view of the labyrinth of St George's Cross Interchange, which begins at Charing Cross. St George's Road, the horizontal street running under the motorway, is now a quiet backwater between two main roads. Great Western Road is the vertical street to the right of the view. Isolated on a gushet between St George's Road, Great Western Road and Maryhill Road is Clarendon Place (1839–41), the only part built of a grand circus planned in the 1830s to mark the junction. Alongside Clarendon Place is a statue of St George and the Dragon. Left of Clarendon Place, across the motorway, is its contemporary, Queen's Crescent.

The curved thoroughfare on the left is Buccleuch Street, where one of its tenements, still with its interior fittings and furnishings of 1911, is the National Trust for Scotland's Tenement House. Just visible in the view bottom centre is the Stow College in Shamrock Street, the city's first purpose-built further education college.

Clarendon Place, the only part built of a development that its architect Alexander Taylor envisaged as one of 'the finest and most spacious approaches to the city'. He intended it to be a grand housing development on the lines of Waterloo Place at the east end of Princes Street, Edinburgh. As was usually the case, however, funds did not permit and the scheme came to a halt.
Courtesy of Glasgow Development and Regeneration Services

Equestrian statue of St George and the Dragon (1897) by J. & G. Mossman. It was originally on the façade of the St George's Cross Co-operative Society, hence the unworked back of the piece. When the building was demolished in 1985, the Co-op presented the statue to the city who erected it on its present site in 1988. The railings around the statue were once around the public convenience at the old cross.
Courtesy of Glasgow Development and Regeneration Services

1. Queen's Crescent
2. Clarendon Place
3. Maryhill Road
4. Great Western Road
5. St George's Road
6. Buccleuch Street
7. Stow College

1. Kelvin Way Bridge
2. Kelvingrove Park
3. River Kelvin
4. Kelvingrove Art Gallery
   and Museum
5. Argyle Street
6. Kelvin Hall
7. Partick Bridge
8. Partick Sewage Pumping Station
9. Royal Hospital for Sick Children

Kelvingrove Art Gallery and Museum and Kelvin Hall 2006

In the centre of the view is the Kelvingrove Art Gallery and Museum, or the Art Galleries to Glaswegians. With its exotic towers, spires, statues and vivid colour, it is their favourite building. Its planning began in 1886 when the city decided to build a combined art gallery and museum to house all its collections under one roof.

The style chosen by the English architects J. W. Simpson and E. J. Milner Allen who won the competition to design the proposed gallery was Spanish Baroque, the centre of the west front being modelled closely on Santiago della Compostella, Obradoiro. In 1901 another international exhibition inaugurated the opening of the building the rich red sandstone colour of which contrasted with James Miller's white and gold oriental-style main exhibition hall, which was nicknamed 'Baghdad on the Kelvin'. It was also one of the first buildings in the west of Scotland to be lit electrically.

It is an oft-told story that the Art Galleries were built back to front in error and that its architect committed suicide by jumping from one of the towers when he realised what had happened. It is a fallacy. The main entrance, the one shown in the view, was planned to face north across the Kelvin Valley. The most used entrance, however, is off Argyle Street, the curving street in the view. After being closed for three years during a £28 million refurbishment, the Art Galleries reopened on 11 July 2006.

On the left-hand side of Argyle Street is the Kelvin Hall, built to replace the previous one, burned down in 1926. The front of the red sandstone building consists of a long main block with tall twin towers terminating in lanterns surmounted by bronze globes, symbolising the building's all-embracing and universal purpose. Before the Scottish Exhibition Conference Centre superseded it, the building was the venue for countless exhibitions, conferences, motor shows and the annual Christmas Carnival and Circus. Throughout the Second World War it was the country's chief factory for the manufacture of sea-rescue dinghies and barrage and convoy balloons. During Billy Graham's 'Tell Scotland Crusade' in 1954 it became a vast auditorium seating 14,000 people.

In 1985 the rear part became the Museum of Transport and the front part the Kelvin Hall International Sports Arena.

Meandering through Kelvingrove Park is the River Kelvin, which flows under Partick Bridge (1876–8), right of the Kelvin Hall in the view. The bridge has four plaques, one at each corner, giving a brief history of its construction. Bottom left, just in the view, is the Kelvin Way Bridge of 1913–14.

This view of the 1901 International Exhibition shows how effectively the exotic white and gold main exhibition hall contrasted with the brilliant red sandstone of the new Kelvingrove Art Gallery and Museum, which served as the Palace of Art during the exhibition. The building was officially opened in 1902. To the right is Glasgow University.

Kelvingrove Park 1966

Crown copyright P1: 58/RAF/7542 0027

This photograph shows the Stewart Memorial Fountain at the 1901 exhibition flanked by Irish cottages used to promote the country's weaving industry. Topping the fountain designed by James Sellars and sculpted by James Mossman is a bronze figure of Sir Walter Scott's Lady of the Lake. Beneath the figure are lions and unicorns holding shields. Roundels feature Zodiac signs, and plaques portray Lord Provost Stewart and scenes commemorating the water supply from Loch Katrine. Behind the fountain is Park Terrace.

This far-reaching view looks over Kelvingrove Park towards Partick. Acquired in 1852, the park occupies the valley where the River Kelvin flows between Gilmorehill and Woodlands Hill. It is the city's most picturesque park and takes its name from the Kelvingrove Estate that formed its nucleus. Initially there was strong opposition to the park as its lack of large flat surfaces made it unsuitable for games. Originally called the West End Park, it was the site for international exhibitions in 1888 and 1901, and in 1911 for the Scottish National Exhibition. Laid out on the steep slopes are walks among trees and statues, with bowling, tennis, etc., located at the flatter areas east of the Art Galleries.

Centre bottom in the view is the Stewart Memorial Fountain, erected in 1872. It commemorates Lord Provost Robert Stewart who was instrumental in bringing Loch Katrine water into Glasgow. Right of the fountain is the ornamental pond with an island shaped like Cyprus. Beyond the pond is the bandstand of 1924, currently under threat of demolition. Far left of the bandstand is the Kelvin Way Bridge.

Centre right in the view is the Western Infirmary, opened in 1874. John Burnet designed the main block (now dwarfed by taller modern additions) in Baronial style, complete with a turreted centre gable supposedly inspired by Glamis Castle. The infirmary has a secret on the first floor, a full-sized church, one of a small handful of churches in the world dedicated to the doctors and nurses who died in both World Wars. Left of the hospital is the only remnant of the 1901 exhibition, the Sunlight Cottages erected as replicas of those at Port Sunlight in Cheshire and given to the city by Lord Leverhulme after the exhibition closed.

Left in the view are the Art Galleries and Kelvin Hall, with Argyle Street between them merging west into Dumbarton Road, which runs through Partick, the area in the top half of the view. In Partick, top centre, is the West of Scotland Cricket Club, the venue for the world's first international football match, held on 30 November 1872 between Scotland and England, Queen's Park providing all the players for the Scottish side. The result was a goalless draw.

1. Stewart Memorial
   Fountain
2. Ornamental Pond
3. Bandstand
4. Roller Skating Rink
5. Kelvin Way Bridge
6. Kelvingrove Art
   Gallery and Museum
7. Argyle Street
8. Kelvin Hall
9. West of Scotland
   Cricket Ground
10. Western Infirmary
11. Sunlight Cottages
12. River Kelvin

1. St Jude's Free Presbyterian Church
2. Lynedoch Crescent
3. Lynedoch Street
4. Lynedoch Place
5. Trinity College and Church
6. Woodside Terrace
7. Claremont Terrace
8. Woodlands Terrace
9. Park Gardens
10. Park Terrace
11. Park Gate
12. Park Quadrant
13. Park Circus
14. Park Circus Place
15. Park Church Tower

Park Circus 1998

Charles Wilson designed the Park area of Woodlands Hill between 1855 and 1863. It is Glasgow's finest example of Victorian town planning on a grand scale, and many consider it unsurpassed in Britain.

Wilson's plan was to follow the area's contour lines and have a central circus at the top of the hill surrounded by outward-facing terraces. He also designed the exteriors of some of the houses, which were exceptionally high-quality mansions for the wealthy.

The development of the hill did not begin with Wilson. Edinburgh architect George Smith laid out the southern slopes in the 1830s and 1840s, and in the lower part of the view is Lynedoch Crescent, which takes up most of one side of Lynedoch Street, the only street that climbs straight up the hill. Behind the crescent is St Jude's Free Presbyterian Church, with Lynedoch Place to its left.

Left of the crescent is the most ambitious of Wilson's buildings – Trinity College and Church, begun in 1855 for the Free Church of Scotland. Three towers, all with very elongated round-arched openings, dominate the design. The tallest one belonged to the college, the two smaller ones to the church. The church was destroyed by fire in 1903 and reconstructed as the college library. The complex is now residential. Right of Trinity is the tower of John Rochead's Park Church, the rest was demolished in 1968. So prominent are the four Park towers on Glasgow's skyline that they have been compared to Tuscany's medieval San Gimignano.

Central in the view is the heart of Wilson's grand plan, Park Circus, entered at the top by Park Gate, from the bottom by Park Circus Place and to the left from Park Street South. The houses were sold as empty shells and the purchasers had to commission architects to design them internally. James Boucher gave No. 22, owned by Walter Macfarlane of the Saracen Foundry, the most sumptuous interior in the West End. The building is now owned by Glasgow City Council and is the country's most magnificent set of marriage rooms.

The outward-facing terraces surrounding the circus are Woodlands to the left, curving into Park, which has French Renaissance-style houses. To the right is the unfinished Park Quadrant.

Far left in the view are Woodside and Claremont Terraces and Park Gardens, No. 6 of which has an interesting past. In 1860 it was bought by John Muir who became Lord Provost in 1889. In 1913 suffragettes nearly burned it down. During the Second World War it was the Glasgow headquarters of the women's branch of the Auxiliary Territorial Service. In 1956 it became the headquarters of the Scottish Football Association. It is now a home again.

The magnificent Italian Renaissance-style arcaded hall of 22 Park Circus. Walter Macfarlane, its owner, spared no expense in its décor, and the house had the most opulent exotic interior in the city, the City Chambers having still to be built. The house had four floors, the ground one having a billiard room, Turkish bath and conservatory. Later, without interfering with Boucher's lavish interior, the house was refurbished by adding some of the finest Glasgow Art Nouveau style, giving it the best of two eras.

Park Circus Fire 2006

When the RCAHMS's photographer Bob Adam was carrying out a sortie over Glasgow on 13 June looking for views for the book, he captured this spectacular shot of a fire in the former University of Glasgow Maclay Hall students' hall of residence in Park Gate in the West End.

The A-listed five-storey Victorian townhouse was being converted into three townhouses when the roof caught fire shortly after midday, not long before this view was taken. By the time the firefighters arrived at the scene, the fire was well advanced, the wind conditions having caused it to spread quickly. When the alarm was raised, workers inside the building were evacuated along with residents in nearby Park Quadrant. Crowds of people in Kelvingrove Park and office workers watched the firefighters trying to control the fire by directing water cannons at it.

Smoke could be seen for miles around as more than sixty firefighters spent over five hours tackling the blaze. As the roof was destroyed and all the interior floors in the building collapsed during the fire, to prevent further damage building control experts shored up the exterior walls. The cost of repairing the building could top £3 million. As to the cause of the fire, one theory is that a worker's blowtorch may have started it.

Near top right in the view are the spectacular four Park towers, three of them belonging to the former Trinity College and Church, the fourth (the white one) to Park Church, the rest of which was demolished in 1968.

University of Glasgow 2005

The University of Glasgow's origins go back to 1451 when Pope Nicholas V granted a papal bull to Bishop William Turnbull to establish a university in the city. The university began in the Cathedral but in the mid-seventeenth century moved to purpose-built premises in High Street where it was known as the Old College. In 1845 the Glasgow, Airdrie and Monklands Railway Company made an offer for the site in return for which it would build a new university on Woodlands Hill. The deal never materialised, but in 1864 an offer from the City of Glasgow Union Railway Company was accepted, whereupon the university acquired a site at Gilmorehill, Woodlands having by then been developed.

On 8 October 1868 the Prince and Princess of Wales, the future King Edward VII and Queen Alexandra, laid the university's foundation stone. Before the ceremony, the first graduation took place when the Prince of Wales and Prince John of Gluckstein received the honorary degree of Doctor of Law.

The photograph shows Glasgow University overlooking Kelvingrove Park. The Gothic-style main building, begun in 1864 by Sir George Gilbert Scott, consists of buildings arranged around two quadrangles separated by the Bute and Randolph Halls, gifted respectively by the third Marquis of Bute and ship-builder Charles Randolph. Adjoining the west quadrangle is Professors' Square, with the Principal's Residence at its south end. Lord Kelvin lived at No. 11 during his long association with the university. The Flemish-style central tower, begun by George Gilbert Scott and finished by his son, J. Oldrid Scott, is a landmark.

Left of the tower is the War Memorial Chapel, erected in memory of the 755 men associated with the university who died in the First World War. West of the Chapel but not in the view is the Lion and Unicorn Staircase of 1690, salvaged from the Old College. Incorporated into Pearce Lodge, centre right in the view, are other reminders of the Old College – the gateway, balcony and coat of arms.

Behind the university in University Avenue is the Roman temple-style Wellington Church of 1882–4 by T. L. Watson, modelled on the Madeleine in Paris. Left of the church is the circular university Reading Room, opened in 1939 and built in the grounds of Hillhead House. Left of the Reading Room is the modern Hunterian Art Gallery whose collection ranges from sixteenth-century paintings to contemporary art. The adjacent Mackintosh House is a reconstruction, inside and out, of Charles and Margaret Mackintosh's house at 78 Southpark Avenue. The tall complex behind the gallery is the University Library of 1968. Top right is the red-brick butterfly-shaped Hillhead High School, one of the once common open-gallery-access Glasgow Corporation schools of the 1930s, recently modernised.

Pearce Lodge in University Avenue contains a reminder of the Old College in High Street, as, thanks to the generosity of shipbuilder Sir William Pearce, fragments of the seventeenth-century entrance front were saved and incorporated into the new university entrance lodge. This photograph clearly shows the old gateway, balcony and coat of arms.

1. Professors' Square
2. Principal's Residence
3. War Memorial Chapel
4. Bute and Randolph Halls
5. Pearce Lodge
6. Wellington Church
7. Reading Room
8. Hunterian Museum and Mackintosh House
9. University Library
10. Hillhead High School

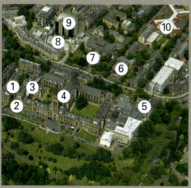

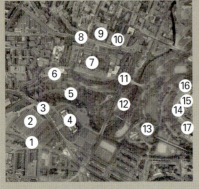

1. Old Dumbarton Road
2. Kelvin Hall
3. Argyle Street
4. Kelvingrove Art
   Gallery and Museum
5. River Kelvin
6. The Western Infirmary
7. Glasgow University
8. University Avenue
9. University Reading
   Room
10. Wellington Church
11. Kelvin Way
12. Bandstand
13. Stewart Memorial
    Fountain
14. Park Terrace
15. Park Gate
16. Park Quadrant
17. Park Gardens

General View of the West End 1979

This drawing by the famous architect Sir Basil Spence shows the Kelvin Hall decked out for an international exhibition in 1949. *Crown copyright RCAHMS ref. SC684959*

At first sight this vertical view of the West End looks a complicated jumble. Closer examination, however, reveals that it encompasses the four previous views and that once the arteries have been identified it is easy to get one's bearings. To begin with, the tree-lined River Kelvin meanders across the view from top right to bottom left.

At centre left the two curved thoroughfares that meet are Argyle Street and Old Dumbarton Road with, in between, the Kelvin Hall, which opened in 1927 and which, before the Scottish Exhibition Conference Centre superseded it, hosted exhibitions and conferences and the annual Christmas Carnival and Circus. Converted into a factory during the Second World War, it manufactured sea-rescue dinghies as well as barrage and convoy balloons.

Right of the Kelvin Hall is the Kelvingrove Art Gallery and Museum, Glaswegians' favourite building and the most visited museum in the UK outside London. It reopened in July 2006 after being closed for three years for refurbishment. To its right are the recreation grounds of Kelvingrove Park. Above the recreation grounds is the bridge leading to Kelvin Way, which runs upwards to the Gothic-style university the two quadrangles of which are easy to make out in the centre of the top half of the view. Below the university to the left is the Western Infirmary. The circular building behind the university in University Avenue is its Reading Room, opened in 1939. To its right is Wellington Church of 1882–4, modelled on the Madeleine in Paris and named after a previous church that was in Wellington Street in the city centre.

Centre right in the view is Park Terrace, Park Quadrant and Park Gate, leading into Park Circus. Below them is Park Gardens. Left of the Park area buildings is Kelvingrove Park, the Stewart Memorial Fountain being within the small circular area. The bandstand is to the left across the River Kelvin and beside Kelvin Way, where a Suffrage Oak to commemorate the granting of votes to women was planted in 1918.

Botanic Gardens 2005

Glasgow's first Botanic Garden was the Physic Garden in the Old College in High Street. Around 1815 the Royal Botanic Institution of Glasgow established the second, near Charing Cross. In 1838, because of rising land values in the area, the Institution sold the site and purchased another in Great Western Road. The new Botanic Gardens opened in 1842 but only for Institution members, as it was a private body. The public was allowed in on Saturdays for one shilling, and occasionally the gardens were 'thrown open to the working classes on the payment of one penny each'. Later the Corporation took over the gardens.

The circular structure in the view is the world-renowned Kibble Palace (in the course of reconstruction), named after the engineer John Kibble who had the magnificent conservatory built at his home in Coulport, Loch Long. Kibble offered the structure to Glasgow for erection in Queen's Park, but, when the city dithered, he withdrew his offer and in 1873 had it moved to the Botanic Gardens where he used the Crystal Art Palace and Conservatory as a concert hall. Meetings were also held there, including rectorial addresses delivered to the University's students by Disraeli. and Gladstone. The photograph shows it being rebuilt after repair of the components. The botanical collection started in 1881, and the Corporation acquired the gardens in 1891. Left of the Palace are the main glasshouses.

To the right in the view is the BBC complex incorporating the former Queen Margaret College, originally the Renaissance palace-style Northpark House designed by John Rochead in 1869 for John Bell, the owner of the Glasgow Pottery at Port Dundas. It has been the property of the BBC since 1938. Queen Margaret Bridge (1926) crosses the River Kelvin.

Crown copyright RCAHMS Ref. DP9906

Hillhead 1991

The construction of Great Western Road, one of Britain's grandest suburban boulevards, led to the development of Glasgow's west end and the lands of Hillhead being expanded into a desirable residential area with a direct route to Glasgow. Previously there were only three ways into Hillhead from Glasgow – by Dumbarton Road and up Byres Road, by crossing Hillhead Bridge at what is now Gibson Street, and by crossing the Kelvin by a low-level bridge below today's Kelvin Bridge.

Building in Hillhead began with mansions such as Hillhead House, Northpark House and Lilybank House. It was not until around 1850 that its acclaimed terraces began to appear, the first and grandest being in Great Western Road.

When the population had risen to 3,654 in 1869, Hillhead became a police burgh under the jurisdiction of the Chief Constable of Lanarkshire at Hamilton. While Hillhead did not at any time form part of 'Old Glasgow', the city annexed it in 1891.

The street bisecting the view is Great Western Road. To its right, from top to bottom, are the Botanic Gardens and the Kibble Palace. Buckingham and Ruskin Terraces come next with, to their right, the BBC complex incorporating the former Queen Margaret College, once Northpark House. Further down, between Hamilton Park Avenue (which curves into La Crosse Terrace) and Belmont Street, is the charming Belmont Crescent of 1869–70 by John Honeyman.

Moving to the left-hand side of Great Western Road, opposite the Botanic Gardens are Belhaven Terrace, Kew Terrace and one of Glasgow's architectural gems, John Rochead's magnificent Venetian style Grosvenor Terrace of 1858. Near Grosvenor Terrace, at the corner of Great Western Road and Byres Road, is Kelvinside Parish Church (1862), which became the Glasgow Bible Training College and is now the Oran Mor cultural centre and meeting place.

Forking left of the church, Byres Road leads southwards to Dumbarton Road and Partick Cross. Right of Byres Road in Saltoun Street is Kelvinside Hillhead Parish Church, modelled on Sainte Chapelle in Paris, which contains some of the finest stained glass in the country by Burne Jones, Cottier and Sadie McLellan.

The area on the left side of Great Western Road below Byres Road is less grand than that to the right as it consists mainly of streets of tenements, such as Cecil and Hillhead Streets. The unusually shaped building middle left is Hillhead High School in Oakfield Avenue.

Great Western Road at Buckingham Terrace in 1950.

Crown copyright RCAHMS Ref. B71317CN

1. BBC Complex
2. Kibble Palace
3. Botanic Gardens
4. Great Western Road
5. Grosvenor Terrace
6. Kelvinside Parish Church
7. Kelvinside Hillhead Parish Church
8. Byres Road
9. Buckingham Terrace
10. Ruskin Terrace
11. Belmont Crescent
12. Hillhead High School

The River Clyde

This view of the Broomielaw reaches north to Port Dundas.
Broomielaw means a grassy slope or meadow with broom
growing on it. The Campus de Bromilaw was mentioned
about 1325. About 1556 the removal of a ford and sandbanks
enabled small craft to reach it. There was no harbour, vessels
simply mooring in mid-stream until the first Broomielaw
Quay was built in the seventeenth century. By the nineteenth
century the Broomielaw was a thriving, bustling waterfront.

The Broomielaw starts west of Jamaica Street and
finishes at the Kingston Bridge. *Courtesy of Clydeport*

1. Weir and Pipe Bridge
2. The Albert Bridge
3. City of Glasgow Union Railway Bridge
4. The Victoria Bridge
5. South Portland Street Suspension Bridge
6. Jamaica Bridge
7. Caledonian Railway Bridge
8. Kingston Bridge
9. Clyde Arc
10. Bell's Bridge
11. Millennium Bridge

The River Clyde and its Bridges 2006

There's an old adage, 'Glasgow made the Clyde, and the Clyde made Glasgow.' This is true. In early times the river was a meandering shallow stream more famous for salmon than for anything else. Glasgow's merchants used Irvine as their shipping port and transported their goods by packhorses to Glasgow.

No practical method of deepening the river was found until 1768 when Chester engineer John Golbourne suggested throwing the current into the centre of the river by means of jetties and helping the natural scour of the water further by dredging the channel. By 1775 the Clyde was navigable, and vessels drawing six feet of water were able to come up to the Broomielaw at high tide for the first time. Thanks to Golbourne, the Clyde had begun to develop into one of the world's finest waterways and ports.

This view of the river looking downstream shows its many bridges. Starting from the bottom, the first is the Tidal Weir. Next, at the foot of Saltmarket, is the Albert Bridge, opened in 1871. Its spandrels bear Glasgow's coat of arms and those of Queen Victoria and Prince Albert, after whom the bridge is named. It is the locality's fifth bridge. The first, Hutchesontown Bridge, was begun in 1794 and destroyed by a flood a year later. Next is the City Union Railway Bridge with, above it, the Victoria Bridge of 1851–4 that replaced Glasgow's medieval bridge of 1345. After that is the South Portland Street suspension footbridge, originally known as 'the halfpenny bridge', the charge first made to cross it.

Next are three bridges close together. The first is Jamaica, or Glasgow, Bridge, built in 1895–9. After that is the Caledonian Railway Bridge of 1899–1905 carrying thirteen railway tracks from Central Station across the river. Beyond the Caledonian Bridge and hidden by it in the view is the King George V Bridge of 1924–7.

Four more bridges follow the KGV. The first is the Kingston Bridge (1970) with a span of 470 feet and a clearance over the river of 60 feet. Second is the new Clyde Arc, nicknamed the Squinty Bridge because it cuts diagonally across the river. Third is Bell's Bridge (1988), built to allow pedestrian access from the north bank to the Garden Festival on the south bank. The bridge opens to allow the passage of shipping up and down the river. Fourth is the Millennium Footbridge connecting the north bank with the Science Centre on the south bank. Another bridge is under way, the Neptune pedestrian and cycle bridge between Tradeston and Anderston. Also proposed is a pedestrian bridge linking Springfield Quay with Lancefield Quay on the north bank.

This postcard of 1920 shows Jamaica Bridge, the third on the site. The first, of 1768–72, called Broomielaw Bridge, was replaced by Thomas Telford's bridge of 1833, which, because it was too narrow, its foundations too shallow and the size of the arches inconvenient for shipping, was replaced by the present seven-arched bridge, almost a replica of Telford's. Left of Jamaica Bridge is the Caledonian Railway Bridge. Upstream are the piers of the original bridge of 1878. The single-decker buses parked in Carlton Place were a 'Pullman' service operated by William J. Wright to Barrhead, Neilston, Dunlop and Kilmarnock.

The Upper Harbour,
the Broomielaw and Kingston Dock 1960

This wonderful drawing of a bustling Broomielaw comes from Stratten's *Glasgow and its Environs*, published in 1891. Horses and carts and carriages ply up and down the quayside with a couple of steam-driven vehicles puffing along amongst them. Goods are piled up outside the sheds. Passengers are embarking on a paddle steamer. Bottom right are the masts of a sailing ship. In the centre are the Jamaica Street and Caledonian Railway Bridges, both replaced by today's bridges. Upriver are the South Portland Street Suspension Bridge, the Victoria Bridge and the Albert Bridge. Top right is the steeple of Gorbals Parish Church. Top left is the Merchants' Steeple.

Central in the view above the three bridges (George V, Caledonian Railway and Jamaica) is the Upper Harbour, or Custom House Quay, opened to shipping in 1852. Extending from Jamaica Bridge to Albert Bridge, most of the quayside was on the north side of the river and chiefly used by vessels in the mineral and coasting trades. A regular sight was steam puffers delivering granite chips. Right of the harbour is the Gorbals, and left the St Enoch Hotel and Station, demolished in the 1970s.

On the left, below the bridges, is the Broomielaw from which the Firth of Clyde pleasure steamers originally sailed. In their heyday, Glasgow Fair Saturday saw thousands leaving the Broomielaw for a trip 'doon the watter', Rothesay the favoured destination. There were several fleet owners, among them David MacBrayne. In 1929 the steamers moved across the river to Bridge Wharf, originally Clyde Place Quay.

The red, blue and black funnelled Burns & Laird Irish Cross Channel steamers berthed at the Broomielaw. Two vessels were needed to provide a daily service to Belfast. Another ship operated the Dublin service.

Direct sailings from Glasgow to Ireland were withdrawn in 1969.

Opposite the Broomielaw is the Kingston Dock, Glasgow's earliest river dock, opened in 1867. It was a small tidal basin of five and a half acres built on the site of a sandpit. A swing bridge worked by steam spanned the entrance. Although it opened as Windmillcroft Basin, it became known as Kingston Dock as the district in which it was situated was Kingston. The quay retained the name of Windmillcroft.

Twenty-two ships of 500 tons could be fitted two deep around the 830 yards of the dock. Some of the early Australian emigrant ships berthed there, with those of the County Line to the Far East and the Allan Line to Canada visiting regularly. Later, mainly coastal vessels used the dock. During improvements in 1914 fire destroyed the wharves and four schooners. To make way for the building of the Kingston Bridge the dock closed in 1966, the last ship to leave it being the *Loch Carron*, owned by David MacBrayne. The dock was later infilled and housing built on the site.

1. The Broomielaw
2. St Enoch Hotel and Station
3. Custom House Quay
4. Victoria Bridge
5. Gorbals
6. Jamaica Bridge
7. George V Bridge
8. Caledonian Railway Bridge
9. Bridge Wharf
10. Kingston Dock
11. Riverside Flour Mills

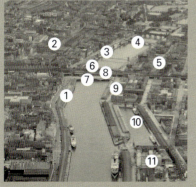

1. Daily Record and Sunday Mail Headquarters
2. Kingston Bridge
3. Tuxedo Princess
4. Former Kingston Dock
5. Bridge Wharf
6. Former Renfrew Ferry
7. Broomielaw
8. Clydeport Building
9. King George V Bridge, Caledonian Railway Bridge and Jamaica Bridge
10. St Enoch Centre

The Kingston Bridge 1989

Crown copyright RCAHMS Ref. B21672CN

While the area in this view of 1989 is identical to the previous one, twenty-nine years have brought changes, the most prominent being the Kingston Bridge, which connects the north and south sections of the M8 motorway. Completed in 1970, it consists of two parallel structures supported by a pier on each quay. It has five lanes each way, and its highest point of 60 feet above high water allows dredgers to pass under it. It is the second busiest river crossing in Europe after the Queen Elizabeth II Bridge that carries London's M25. Moored alongside the bridge is the *Tuxedo Princess* nightclub ship, a former Stranraer-Larne car ferry. Right of the ship, now departed, is a housing development in place of the Kingston Dock.

At the bottom left edge of the view is the headquarters of the *Daily Record* and *Sunday Mail* at Anderston Quay, the most visible newspaper office in the country when it opened in 1971. Launched in 1900 as the first halfpenny morning newspaper in the United Kingdom, the *Record* was the first daily paper to colour-print at speed and the first national daily to be put together with the help of computers. In 2000 it moved into state-of-the art headquarters at One Central Quay, just down the road from its Anderston Quay building,

now demolished. The *Record* has had two other homes, the first designed by Charles Rennie Mackintosh in Renfield Lane, the second in Hope Street where, from the outside through its enormous windows, the giant presses were visible churning out the papers.

Instead of transit sheds lining the Broomielaw, as in the previous view, there is a landscaped walkway stretching to Anderston Quay. Many of the buildings left of the quayside have been demolished to make way for the development of the city's newest commercial centre, Atlantic Quay. Having lost its neighbours, the Clydeport building in Robertson Street, partly obscured in the 1960 view, stands out. The splendour of the building, begun in 1882 and extended in 1908, signified that the Clyde Navigation Trust rivalled what was then Glasgow Corporation in power and influence. Beyond Clydeport, the massive St Enoch Shopping Centre has replaced the St Enoch Hotel and Station. The vessel at Bridge Wharf (still with its low long transit sheds) is the former Renfrew Ferry converted into an entertainment centre and now moored on the opposite bank of the river to make way for the construction of the Broomielaw/Tradeston pedestrian bridge.

This superb photograph shows the Kingston Bridge in progress in the late 1960s. Centre right is the Kingston Dock, not yet filled in and with its transit sheds intact. The buildings bottom right, now demolished, are grain mills belonging to the firm of Joseph Rank & Sons. Across the river, the Broomielaw also still has its sheds. *Simmons Aerofilms*

Finnieston Ferry and Harbour Tunnel 1930

This stunning ground view of 2005 of the same area as opposite shows changes. The Seamen's Restaurant has gone, as have the warehouses, now replaced by the City Inn and housing. While the rotunda is still there, it is now a casino. The biggest change, however, is that the Finnieston Crane now dominates the skyline around Stobcross Quay. Apparently, it was so large that an enthusiastic stevedore said: 'You can ride a bicycle round the jib up there.' It could lift 175 tons at a time and was erected specifically for loading railway locomotives on to cargo vessels. During Mayfest in 1987, George Wylie's straw locomotive was dangled from the crane, symbolising its industrial past. Unlike the other four Titan cranes on the river, it was built by Cowans, Sheldon & Co. Ltd of Carlisle, not William Arrol. It is listed as an industrial monument.
Courtesy of Clydeport

As Glasgow expanded west on both banks of the river, there was a growing need to increase cross-river access, and as bridges would have restricted ship access to the Broomielaw, ferries were introduced. Initially these were no more than broad rowing boats, but following the upturning of one of these in 1864 when nineteen people drowned, the Clyde Trust introduced a steam passenger service in 1865. The three major ferries were the Govan Ferry, the Whiteinch Ferry and the Finnieston Ferry.

The ferry landing stage in the view divides Finnieston Quay from Stobcross Quay – Finnieston to the right, Stobcross to the left. Docked is an elevating vehicular deck ferry, first introduced in 1890 between Finnieston and Mavisbank Quay. The carrying deck, which could be raised and lowered by fourteen feet to align with the quay, accommodated eight carts and horses and 300 passengers. There were four such ferries on the river, the last being withdrawn at Finnieston in 1966. To the right of the ferry, leading down to the river, is the steep stairway used to access the passenger ferries visible beside the landing stage on the opposite bank. These ferries continued until 1977.

The lattice-girder tower being erected left of the ferry was to support the giant cantilever Finnieston Crane, finished in 1931 and described as the new electric crane.

The rotunda behind the ferry was the northern entrance to the Harbour Tunnel built in 1890–96. There was a twin on the south bank. The tunnel ran south from Finnieston under the river to Mavisbank Quay in Govan. Inside the rotundas, an 80-foot vertical shaft gave access to three tunnels, two for vehicular traffic (then horse-drawn vehicles) and one for pedestrians who shared it with a water main. Access for carts was by hydraulic lifts. For pedestrians it was by stairs. Although the tunnels were lit by electricity, it could be quite frightening going through them as the clattering hooves of the horses echoed loudly in the confined space. Used until 1943 for traffic and until 1980 for passengers, the tunnels have been infilled, with access to the water mains maintained. The white building to the left of the rotunda is the Seamen's Restaurant.

1. Passenger Ferries
2. Stobcross Quay
3. Finnieston Crane Tower
4. Vehicular Ferry
5. Finnieston Quay
6. Finnieston Harbour
   Tunnel Rotunda
7. Seamen's Restaurant
8. Finnieston Street

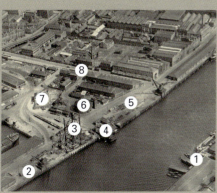

The Clyde Arc
(the Squinty Bridge) 2006

From ferries and harbour tunnels to Glasgow's newest bridge. This view shows the Clyde Arc, nicknamed the Squinty Bridge because it cuts diagonally across the river. It is the first road bridge to be built over the Clyde since the Kingston Bridge opened in 1970. It links Finnieston Street on the north bank with Govan Road on the south and provides access to Pacific Quay (the former Prince's Dock) where the Science Centre is situated and where the BBC's new headquarters are nearing completion. Scottish Television has already relocated to the quay.

The Squinty Bridge has two lanes in each direction, one for cars, the other for taxis and buses. It also has pedestrian and cycle paths. It was not a new idea to build a bridge at this point of the river. It was proposed as far back as the early 1930s, the intention being to retire the harbour tunnel.

Middle right in the view is the Prince's Dock hydraulic pumphouse of 1893–4. At its south end is the stump of an octagonal chimney in the form of the 'Tower of the Winds', with sculptured panels forming the frieze. During the Garden Festival of 1988 (constructed on the infilled Prince's Dock) the pumphouse became the Four Winds Restaurant. Left of the pumphouse is the south rotunda, with across the river its twin and the Finnieston Crane, left of which is the City Inn. Modern housing on each side of the river complements the Squinty Bridge.

Crown copyright RCAHMS Ref. DP9927

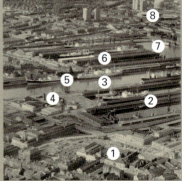

1. Finnieston
2. Queen's Dock
3. River Clyde
4. Finnieston Harbour
   Tunnel Rotunda
5. Finnieston Crane
6. Prince's Dock
7. Canting Basin
8. Ibrox Stadium

Queen's Dock and Prince's Dock 1966

Although Kingston Dock closed in the year this photograph was taken, as can be seen, Queen's Dock and Prince's Dock were still widely used.

Queen's Dock is on the right of the river in the view. Opened in 1877 at Stobcross on the north bank, it was Glasgow's second dock and a major feat of civil engineering. It had 10,000 feet of quay, two basins and a hydraulic powered swing bridge. The Anchor Line ship *Victoria* was the first to enter the dock.

While to begin with the dock accommodated many of the major companies using the original Glasgow Harbour (now Atlantic Quay), such as the Clan and City Lines, later it provided berthage to passenger and cargo ships sailing to Australia, Canada, East Africa, Burma, the West Indies, South America and the Mediterranean. The ships of P. Henderson & Co., commonly known as Paddy Henderson, berthed in the north basin. The company specialised in the trade between Britain and Burma, and the names of its ships were fitting – *Chindwin, Burma, Amarapoora*, etc.

Three years after this photograph was taken the dock closed and was later infilled. Left of the dock is the Finnieston Crane and the Finnieston Harbour Tunnel rotunda. In front of the dock is Finnieston where work has started on clearing the area to make way for the Clyde Expressway.

On the south bank of the river, in Govan, is Prince's Dock (originally Cessnock Dock), built on the lands of Cessnock. This extensive dock complex finished in 1897, had three basins and a canting (turning) basin. The south quay was solely devoted to mineral traffic. Big four-masted barques home from Australia with bagged wheat in their holds berthed in the south basin.

Among the lines using the dock in the inter-war years was the Donaldson Line, which ran services from Glasgow to Canada. Its *Athenia*, built by Fairfield in 1926, was the first ship sunk after the outbreak of the Second World War – seven hours after the official declaration on 3 September 1939. A U-boat torpedoed her off the Irish Coast with the loss of 112 lives. At the time of this view, the ships in the dock were general cargo vessels that sailed to South and East Africa, India, Pakistan, the Persian Gulf, east and west Canada, South America, Sweden and the Great Lakes.

Except for the canting basin, Prince's Dock was infilled in the late 1970s and became the site of the Glasgow Garden Festival in 1988.

This photograph of 1950 clearly shows Queen's Dock's two basins. At the entrance is its hydraulic swing bridge, left of which is the hydraulic pumphouse of 1877 that supplied high-pressure water to the bridge, cranes and capstans. (Prince's Dock also had a pumphouse.) In front of the pumphouse in Yorkhill Quay is an Anchor Line vessel. Right of the dock entrance is the Harbour watchtower, a skeleton framework with a small square hut with a signal arm towering above it. From it, information was conveyed about ships on the river, their positions and times of passing being recorded on a blackboard and later transcribed into a desk book. *Crown copyright RCAHMS PFFO 58/A/436 0058*

Scottish Exhibition and Conference Centre and the Clyde Auditorium 1998

This view shows the Scottish Exhibition and Conference Centre and the Clyde Auditorium (nicknamed 'the Armadillo') built on the former Queen's Dock on the north bank of the river. The City of Glasgow acquired the dock from the Clyde Port Authority in 1976 and started infilling it late in 1977. Much of the infilling material came from demolished tenements, St Enoch Hotel and Station and Cathcart Castle.

The massive shed-like SECC opened in 1985 and was built to replace the Kelvin Hall, which had become unsuitable for modern large-scale events. Covering an area of 19,000 square feet, the centre has five inter-linked halls of varying sizes, the largest being the concert auditorium/conference venue. The centre is capable of housing simultaneously various individual events or one huge gathering, like a pop concert for 12,000 people. When the annual Christmas Carnival and Circus was transferred from the Kelvin Hall, special drains were installed to cope with the elephants.

On the right of the SECC is the eye-catching Clyde Auditorium of 1997. Its nickname, the Armadillo, comes from its shape, composed of a series of large curved ribbed shells covered in aluminium sheeting. It has become an important icon in Glasgow, and many liken it to Sydney's Opera House. Designing the structure was so complex that it involved the production of over 4,000 drawings detailed in such a way as to allow a very fast rate of steelwork erection. The auditorium seats up to 3,200 people on three levels, and the lack of columns allows a free and unobstructed view of the stage. The building is a testimony to the skills of many engineers and craftsmen, and reflects the enterprise for which the city was renowned.

Left of the Armadillo is the slim 20-storey Moat House Hotel, built in 1989. Originally called the Forum, it is one of the most striking buildings in the city, being totally clad in highly reflecting silver-blue mirrored glass.

Spanning the river is Bell's Bridge, named after its whisky firm sponsor and built to allow pedestrian access from the north bank to the Garden Festival site – the infilled Prince's Dock.

This unusual view of Finnieston Quay looks upriver. On the left is the former Queen's Dock hydraulic pumphouse, now the Clyde Maritime Centre. Alongside is the Tall Ship, the *Glenlee*, a steel-hulled sailing ship built in Port Glasgow in 1896 and one of only five nineteenth-century Clyde-built sailing ships still afloat. The ship is open to visitors. The Armadillo comes after the *Glenlee*, with the Moat House Hotel beside it. In front of the hotel is Glasgow's heliport. Operations from here include private flying, emergency air services, pleasure trips and 'spy in the sky' flights for traffic reports. The Strathclyde Police helicopter with its video and infrared cameras is based here. *Courtesy of Clydeport*

1. Clyde Expressway
2. Scottish Exhibition and
   Conference Centre
3. Moat House Hotel
4. Bell's Bridge
5. The Clyde Auditorium
   ('the Armadillo')

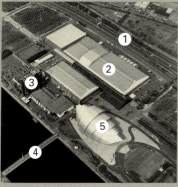

1. Four Winds Restaurant
2. Bell's Bridge
3. Victorian High Street
4. Rendezvous Point
5. Marina
6. Clydesdale Bank Tower
7. Scottish Exhibition and
   Conference Centre
8. Finnieston Crane
9. North Rotunda

The Garden Festival 1988

Courtesy of Glasgow Development and Regeneration Services

This view shows Glasgow's Garden Festival, created on the former Prince's Dock, previously abandoned and derelict, a relic of the city's industrial past. It took three years to transform it into the Garden Festival. After the dock had been filled in, thousands of tons of soil were imported into it. After that, around 300,000 trees and shrubs, and 400,000 feet of turf were planted to form the garden into which went entertainment centres, leisure pavilions, themed gardens, restaurants and fun fairs.

Bell's Bridge, spanning the river in the middle of the view, gave pedestrian access to the festival from the north bank. It led to the entrance gates and a Victorian-style bandstand (borrowed from Rutherglen's Overtoun Park) at the head of the Victorian High Street, the design of which incorporated five towers based on some of the most famous spires in the city, like the Tolbooth, Trinity College and Glasgow University. As well as eating places, the High Street had around twenty shops. The area within the circle was the Rendezvous Point from which the various attractions radiated. Popular with visitors were trips around the bay in a Mississippi steamboat, rides in tramcars and on the little 'steam' railway circling the western end of the site. The Coca-Cola Roller Coaster was also a crowd-puller.

Left in the view is the marina, the former Prince's Dock canting basin with, soaring above it, the 240-foot high Clydesdale Bank Tower the glass cabin of which revolved and rose simultaneously, allowing fantastic views over the whole Glasgow area.

Near middle right in the view is the Four Winds Restaurant, Prince's Dock's former hydraulic pump-house. Across the river is the Scottish Exhibition and Conference Centre with, to its right, the Finnieston Crane and the north rotunda.

Left. This photograph shows the *Waverley*, the world's only seagoing paddle steamer, built by A. & J. Inglis, passing Bell's Bridge and the Garden Festival in 1988. The bridge, built to allow pedestrian access from the north bank to the Festival on the south bank, opens to allow the passage of shipping up and down the river. The part of the Garden Festival shown is the Bell's Bridge entrance, which led to the Victorian style bandstand. Beyond the bandstand is the Victorian High Street with its five multi-coloured stylised towers. On the right is the former Renfrew Ferry.

Below. The Garden Festival symbol

Glasgow Science Centre 2005

To the fury of Glaswegians, when the Garden Festival ended, it was dismantled, with the exception of Bell's Bridge. The site then lay derelict until the Glasgow Science Centre was built on it. Opened in 2001, it consists of three stunning buildings – the crescent-shaped Science Mall, the IMAX Theatre, which looks like a giant golf ball, and the Millennium, or Glasgow Tower. The Mall and the theatre are the only buildings in Europe, apart from Bilbao's Guggenheim, to be clad in shimmering titanium.

There are four floors in the Science Mall, three with individual themes – Exploration, Discovery, Creativity and Innovation. The IMAX Theatre projects 3D films on to a massive 80 x 60 feet screen – the size of a five-storey tenement block. The projector's bulb is so strong it could be seen from the moon. The tower is the only one in the world that completely turns from the ground up. Two glass elevators take visitors to the viewing cabin, saving a leg climb of 500 stairs. In the entrance to the tower there are three pods at the base focusing on Glasgow in the seventeenth, eighteenth and nineteenth centuries, the idea being that people can experience the city in the past. Unfortunately, since its erection the tower has been beset with problems and has been closed more often than it has been open.

STV has relocated to the former Prince's Dock area (now named Pacific Quay), and although the BBC will not move into its new headquarters east of the Science Centre until 2007 (top right in this view), already the site has been dubbed Scotland's 'media village'. The SECC and the Moat House Hotel are across from the Science Centre. Looking upriver is the Millennium Bridge and Bell's Bridge.

Yorkhill Quay 1974

This aerial view of 1931 shows the Anchor Line's *California* and *Cameronia* at the company's berth at Yorkhill Quay. They are facing downriver ready for departure. Behind them are the transit sheds. On the left is Yorkhill Basin where the Anchor Line Indian ships berthed. Across the river from Yorkhill Quay are the Govan Graving Docks with, to their left, part of Harland & Wolff's ship-yard.

This view shows Yorkhill Quay with the newly built Clyde Expressway running alongside. The quay ran downriver for two or three hundred yards from the Queen's Dock entrance. It opened in 1909 and became the centre for the North American passenger and cargo trade. The main company to berth at the quay was the Anchor Line whose weekly sailing to New York carried many emigrants. The line's Indian service vessels berthed in the basin right of the transit sheds. Beyond the basin the River Kelvin flows under the Expressway into the Clyde. To meet demands the company built five large liners – *Caledonia, Transylvania, California, Cameronia* and *Tuscania* – in the 1920s. The New York passenger service was withdrawn in 1959, the Indian in 1966.

The cruiser *Sussex* was bombed by a Luftwaffe plane in the basin in 1940. She had come into the Clyde to have a turbine rebladed and was preparing to sail on the morning of 18 September when at 2.40 a.m. a 250-pound bomb crashed through her deck, setting fire to the oil fuel and threatening the magazine. Several of the crew were killed and over 2,000 residents in the neighbourhood and patients in the nearby children's hospital were evacuated. It took firemen twelve hours to control the intense flames. The Govan vehicular ferry No. 4, skilfully manoeuvred alongside the *Sussex*, was used as a platform for firefighting equipment, enabling the cruiser's magazine to be flooded, thus preventing a fatal explosion. It took Alexander Stephen's Linthouse yard two years to rebuild the *Sussex*. There was another spectacular fire at the quay when in 1960 a huge shed containing 46,000 cases of whisky burned down.

Latterly Yorkhill Quay was used for laid-up vessels, with many of the sheds being converted for other roles, such as an antiques warehouse that went on fire in 2005, while the sheds were being demolished to allow for the continuing regeneration of the new Glasgow Harbour area.

Although the quay is not active, until recently visiting Royal Navy vessels berthed there, the crews liking its close proximity to the pleasures of the West End. Presently it is the base for the Clyde Maritime Trust and its sailing ship, *Glenlee*, built in 1896 and the only Clyde-built sailing ship still afloat in Britain. The former Queen's Dock hydraulic pumphouse in the forefront of the view is the Trust's Visitor Centre, offering frequently changing exhibitions, a shop and café. On the promontory left of the centre is the former Harbour watchtower, now demolished.

In the Glasgow Harbour Scheme, Yorkhill Quay is to be developed for retail and leisure use, including a new Museum of Transport.

1. Former Harbour Watchtower
2. Former Hydraulic Pumphouse
3. Yorkhill Quay
4. Transit Sheds
5. Clyde Expressway
6. Yorkhill Basin
7. River Kelvin

1. Prince's Dock
2. Queen's Dock
3. Yorkhill Quay
4. Pointhouse Shipyard and
   Ferry Terminal
5. Govan Vehicular Ferry
6. Harland & Wolff's Govan
   Shipyard
7. Govan Graving Docks

Govan Graving Docks
and Harland & Wolff's Shipyard 1950

This view looking upriver shows Yorkhill Quay, Queen's Dock and Prince's Dock. It also shows the Govan Graving Docks and Harland & Wolff's shipyard.

The graving, or dry docks, are directly opposite Yorkhill Quay. They were a necessary part of harbour facilities and were used for fitting out ships and for ship repairs. While the harbour's first dry dock was opened in 1858 by shipbuilders Tod & MacGregor on the west bank of the River Kelvin, the main public docks were the three built by the Clyde Navigation Trust between 1869 and 1889. The site of the docks was originally that of Govan's first Free Church. The docks closed in 1988.

Downriver from the docks is Harland & Wolff's shipyard, one of the most significant of the Glasgow yards. The Belfast-based shipbuilders took over three existing Govan yards in 1912 and turned them into one, beginning a fifty-year period as marine engineers and shipbuilders, concentrating on building naval vessels, tankers and cargo ships. Although the yard weathered the inter-war years, after a period of decline it closed in 1962, capital investment in new plant and machinery having been concentrated on the company's Belfast yard.

Two ferries are crossing the river, the one on the right being the Govan vehicular ferry about to reach its landing stage at Water Row, which had Harland & Wolff sheds either side of it. A passenger ferry is nearing Pointhouse on the opposite bank.

While this view of 2005 covers the same area as that opposite, it is much changed. The docks have been filled in. The SECC and the Armadillo stand on Queen's Dock, and the Glasgow Science Centre is on Prince's Dock. Two new bridges span the river. Looking upriver, the first is the Millennium Bridge, the next Bell's Bridge. The Govan Graving Docks are now derelict and houses have replaced Harland & Wolff's shipyard. Yorkhill Quay doesn't look very different, but the ship berthed there is not an Anchor Line one, it's the Clyde Maritime Trust's *Glenlee*. Another change is that there are no ferries crossing between Pointhouse and Govan.
*Crown copyright RCAHMS
Ref. DP9598*

Meadowside and Merklands Quays 1930

In the foreground of the view is D. & W. Henderson's Meadowside shipyard, which owed its origins to the firm of Tod & McGregor who began shipbuilding on the south bank of the river in 1838 and in 1844 moved across the river to Meadowside. After the Tod & McGregor period, Handyside & Henderson, the founders of the Anchor Line, acquired the business. Subsequently the name was changed to D. & W. Henderson, which continued shipbuilding in the yard until 1935. Repair work continued until 1965. Apart from building Anchor Line vessels and Clyde steamers, the yard specialised in large yachts like *Britannia*, built in 1893 for the Prince of Wales, later Edward VII.

Downriver from the shipyard is Meadowside Quay where the Clyde Navigation Trust built a granary in 1914. While ships from many countries used it, it was intended for the storing of Canadian grain imported for the local whisky distilleries. The granary, extended twice, was said to contain twenty million bricks and to be the largest brick-built building in Europe. It closed in 1995 and was demolished in 2003 to make way for houses as part of the Glasgow Harbour development.

It was one of the river's great landmarks.

Alongside Meadowside is Merklands Quay, a lairage constructed in 1907 to handle the importation of livestock into the city. Burns & Laird landed large consignments of cattle from Ireland. The lairage closed in 1974 and has now been demolished.

Downriver of Merklands is Barclay Curle's Clydeholm shipyard, the origins of which go back to the earliest days of shipbuilding on the Clyde when in 1818 John Barclay began building sailing ships at Stobcross. The company expanded and in 1855 built another yard at Whiteinch that in 1874 became its sole premises. In 1912 Tyneside shipbuilders Swan Hunter took over Barclay Curle. Shipbuilding at Clydeholm ceased in 1967.

Castlebank Street, continuing as South Street, runs behind Meadowside, Merklands and Clydeholm shipyard. The area in the bottom right-hand quarter of the view is Partick. Whiteinch and Victoria Park are in the top quarter.

On the south bank of the river are the shipyards of Fairfield and Stephen's, which are covered below.

The same scene as that opposite, seventy-five years later. Henderson's shipyard has gone, housing has been built on Meadowside Quay, the granary and the lairage have gone, Barclay Curle's shipyard has gone, as has Stephen's shipyard. All that remains is the former Fairfield Shipyard, now owned by BAE Systems. The Clyde Expressway now runs behind Castlebank/South Streets.

Crown copyright RCAHMS Ref. DP9572

1. Meadowside Shipyard
2. Meadowside Quay
3. Meadowside Granary
4. Merklands Quay
   and Lairage
5. Barclay Curle's
   Clydeholm Shipyard
6. King George V Dock
7. Alexander Stephen's
   Linthouse Shipyard
8. Fairfield Shipyard

1. Elder Park
2. Former Engine Works
3. Fitting-out Basin
4. Titan Crane
5. Fabrication Shed
6. Building berths

Govan Shipyard 2005

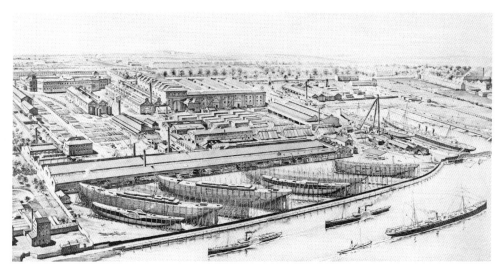

This engraving shows the Fairfield Shipbuilding & Engineering Co. Limited in 1890, looking rather different from the yard of today. Two large liners sit in the fitting-out basin, there are no cranes and the stocks are filled with ships in various stages of construction, one of them a paddle steamer. *Courtesy of BAe Systems*

Govan has a long history of shipbuilding that began in 1839 when Macarthur and Alexander set up a yard on ground east of the Water Row. This view shows the only yard left. It has had many identities, the first being as Randolph Elder & Company, set up in 1864 by Charles Randolph and John Elder on part of Fairfield Farm. The first four vessels built at the yard were blockade-runners for the Confederates to run the Union blockade of the Southern ports during the American Civil War.

When Randolph retired in 1868 and Elder died in 1869 a new partnership headed by William Pearce ran the firm, renamed John Elder & Company. Pearce created a new class of liners that combined luxury with speed. The first of these 'Atlantic Greyhounds', the *Arizona* for the Guion Line, won the coveted Blue Riband awarded for the fastest time between Britain and New York. The Guion *Alaska* and *Oregon*, the Cunarders *Umbria*, *Etruria*, *Campania* and *Lucania* followed the *Arizona*.

The strangest ship built by the yard was *Livadia* – a turbot-shaped yacht for the Tsar of Russia based on a circular battleship design invented by the Russian Admiral Popoff. (To judge how odd the vessel looked there is a model of it in the Transport Museum.) To allow the firm to compete for Admiralty contracts, Pearce converted it into a limited company – the Fairfield Shipbuilding & Engineering Co.

During the First World War Fairfield built passenger and cargo ships as well as warships but in the Second World War (by which time Lithgow owned it) it undertook naval work exclusively, producing thirty ships the most famous of which being the battleship *Howe* and the aircraft carrier *Implacable*.

In 1968 Fairfield became part of the unsuccessful Upper Clyde Shipbuilders. In 1972 it reappeared as part of Govan Shipbuilders, which limped along until the government nationalised it in 1977. In 1988 it became Kvaerner Govan Ltd when a Norwegian concern took it over. Today BAe Systems Marine owns it.

The large white building is the fabrication shed built by Kvaerner. To its right is the fitting-out basin with alongside it a Titan hammerhead crane constructed by William Arrol in 1911 and then the largest crane in the world. Despite being a listed structure, it is under threat of demolition as it might obstruct future development of the yard. Presently a fleet of six Type 45 destroyers is being built at the Govan and Scotstoun sister yards. They will be the biggest warships built in Britain for many years and will keep the yards busy for at least ten years. Behind the shipyard is Elder Park, originally Fairfield Farm, donated by Isabella Elder in memory of her husband, John.

Alexander Stephen & Sons
Linthouse Shipyard 1940

Crown copyright Ref: G287

This view, taken during the Second World War, shows three busy shipyards – Fairfield, Barclay Curle and Stephen's. As Fairfield and Barclay Curle have featured previously, Stephen's is the subject here. The origin of the firm goes back to 1851 when Alexander Stephens came to Glasgow from Burghead and took over Kelvinhaugh Shipyard. In 1869 he bought Linthouse Estate and laid out twenty of its thirty acres as a ship-

yard and workshops. The remainder was reserved for houses for employees and expansion. Linthouse mansion house became the firm's headquarters. In 1878–79 Stephen's built four ships for the newly formed Clan Line, the first being the *Clan Alpine*, followed by the *Clan Fraser*, the *Clan Gordon* and the *Clan Lamont*.

Disaster hit the yard in 1883 when the *Daphne*, built for the Laird Line's Irish trade capsized and sank at her launch. On board were around 200 men still working on the vessel. Of these, 146 drowned.

From 1904 to 1949 Stephen's built magnificent ships for Elders & Fyffes for the banana trade, giving rise to the well-known Glasgow expression, 'Dae ye think ah came up the Clyde oan a banana boat?'

The yard was fortunate during the depression as work from T. and J. Brocklebank, the New Zealand Steamship company and its associate, the Federal Steam Navigation Company Ltd, kept its repair yard busy, making it possible to retain a nucleus of skilled men who were available when war began in 1939. During the war the yard executed 471 Admiralty repair contracts. The most important repair job, however, was that of the cruiser HMS *Sussex*, which had been set on fire and sunk on 18 September 1940 by a Luftwaffe bomb while in Yorkhill Quay for repair. The repair, almost a rebuilding, took two years. As well as carrying out repairs, Stephens supplied the Royal Navy with cruisers, destroyers, minesweepers, corvettes, the aircraft-carrier *Ocean* and the sloop *Amethyst*.

The end of Stephen's as an independent yard and the end of shipbuilding at Linthouse came in 1968 when it became part of Upper Clyde Shipbuilders Ltd.

Directly across the river from Stephen's is Barclay Curle's Clydeholm shipyard, with Merklands and Meadowside Quays to its right. Fairfield shipyard is opposite Meadowside granary.

Top. HMS *Sussex* bombed and sunk in Glasgow Harbour on 18 September 1940.
Left. The refitted *Sussex* restored to active service in 1942.

1. Fairfield Shipyard
2. Meadowside Granary
3. Merklands Quay and Lairage
4. Barclay Curle's Clydeholm Shipyard
5. Shieldhall Sewage Works
6. Alexander Stephen's Linthouse Shipyard
7. Southern General Hospital

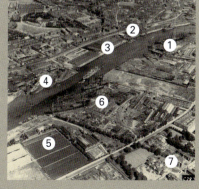

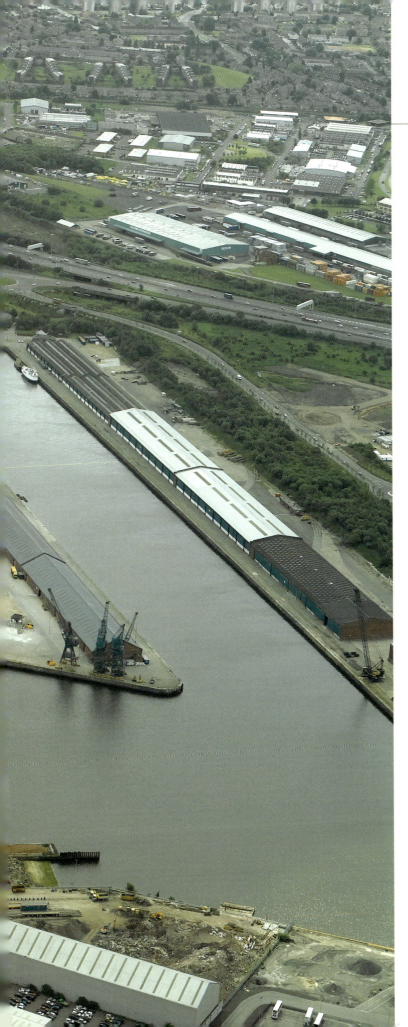

King George V Dock 2006

King George V Dock was the last of the Clyde's docks to be built. King George V, who sailed downriver from Bridge Wharf (just below King George V Bridge) on the turbine steamer *King George V*, opened it in 1931. Unlike the Queen's and Prince's Docks it was a vast single basin with unrestricted entry.

While initially the dock was not used as much as was hoped because of the world depression, its expanse and deep water proved a godsend during the Second World War when it was one of the country's most used shipping facilities.

In May 1942 the United States aircraft carrier USS *Wasp* berthed at the dock where it took on board fifty-seven Spitfire fighter planes for transportation to within flying distance of Malta. As an attack on the island developed when the *Wasp* was fifty miles away, the Spitfires took off, swooped on the attackers and practically wiped them out.

Today the King George V Dock is the main port for Glasgow and the west of Scotland. It handles a wide range of international cargoes, including animal feeds, grain, aggregates, and timber and glass products. It has extensive shed accommodation, paved areas for marshalling cargoes and a comprehensive range of handling equipment.

Just in the view, middle left, is Shieldhall Sewage Works, opened in 1910. Left of the dock across the river is the former North British Diesel Engine Works, built in 1912, with beside it one of the Clyde's five remaining Titan cranes. Known as the Whiteinch Hammerhead, it was the fourth and last Titan built by William Arrol. *Crown copyright RCAHMS Ref. DP9925*

1. Fitting out Basin
2. John Brown's Shipyard
3. Rothesay Dock
4. Coal-loading Hoists
5. Ore handling Cranes

John Brown's Shipyard and Rothesay Dock 1950

Crown copyright RCAHMS SFFO 58/A/436 0022

In the forefront of the view is the yard of John Brown Shipbuilding & Engineering Company, undoubtedly the Clyde's most famous name. Its beginnings lay in the Clydebank Shipyard of J. & G. Thomson, eventually taken over by Sheffield steelmakers John Brown & Company in 1899. The yard had two significant advantages – its building berths were capable of being extended and could be aligned with the mouth of the River Cart on the opposite bank, providing additional launching space for larger ships.

After modernisation, the yard began by building three magnificent liners for the Cunard Line – the *Saxonia*, *Carmania* and *Caronia*. Then came the *Lusitania*, sunk on 3 May 1915 off the coast of southern Ireland by the U-20 German submarine, with the loss of 1,200 lives.

The yard built naval vessels during the First World War, the most famous being the battleship HMS *Hood*, launched in August 1918, too late for service in that war. The 'mighty *Hood*', as she was known, served in the Second World War but during an engagement with the German battleship *Bismarck* on 24 May 1941, her ammunition magazine was struck, the explosion bursting her in two. She sank instantly with the loss of all but three members of her crew of 1,400.

With the collapse of Admiralty work in the 1920s, John Brown's suffered, and work was suspended in 1931 with ship No. 534 under construction. Work on the ship resumed in April 1934, and on 26 September 1934 she was launched as *Queen Mary*, then the greatest liner to grace the ocean. Her sister ship, *Queen Elizabeth*, was launched in 1938. HMS *Vanguard*, the last British battleship built, was launched in 1944, the Royal Yacht *Britannia* in 1953, and *Queen Elizabeth II* in 1967. By a strange coincidence, the name of the designer of the three queens was John Brown.

Brown's yard was part of Upper Clyde Shipbuilders Ltd from 1968 to 1971, when it failed and Marathon of Texas took over to produce oil rigs. When Marathon withdrew, the French UIE Shipbuilding moved in. Closure came in 1997.

Behind the shipyard is Rothesay Dock, which marks the end of Glasgow Harbour. It opened in 1907 to handle coal, ore and mineral shipments and had miles of railway sidings serving four electric coal-loading hoists and various cranes. Today the dock has various uses, such as the new River Clyde Boatyard.

The *Queen Mary* leaving the Clyde en route for Southampton. She made her maiden voyage on 27 May 1936 on the Southampton-Cherbourg-New York route. In 1939 she was converted into a troopship. After making her last transatlantic crossing on 16 September 1967, she was sold to the town of Long Beach, California, where she became a hotel and conference centre. Today she is up for sale, and there are hopes that she will come back to Britain, although there is controversy as to whether it should be to her home port of Southampton or her birthplace, the Clyde.

Second World War River View 1941

This wartime view shows Glasgow Harbour between the Queen's and Prince's Docks and King George V Dock. The description of the view works its way down the right-hand side of the river and up the left. It starts at the top with Prince's Dock, mainly used for cargo trade. After that are the Govan Graving Docks and Harland & Wolff's shipyard, with a barrage balloon to its left. Next is Fairfield shipyard, which undertook naval work exclusively during the war. After Fairfield is Alexander Stephen's shipyard, which not only produced some of the world's finest vessels but had an extensive repair business. Beside Stephen's are the settling tanks of Shieldhall Sewage Works. The view ends just at the corner of King George V Dock, which, because of its expanse and deep water, was a boon during the war as it could accommodate large vessels.

On the left river bank, first, is Charles Connell's shipyard, which closed in 1930 and re-opened in 1937 when the depression was over. After Connell's is the North British Diesel Engine Works of 1914, with a roof that could slide open so that the Titan crane at the quayside could lift the marine engines directly from the works on to ships.

Barclay Curle's Clydeholm shipyard is next, the firm's origins going back to the earliest days of ship-building on the Clyde. It was originally in Stobcross but moved to Whiteinch in 1855 when its site was required for the construction of Queen's Dock. The launch of the *City of Glasgow* in 1848 at Stobcross was such an important event that a public holiday was held.

After Barclay Curle is Meadowside Quay with its massive granary. Beyond the quay is D. & W. Henderson's shipyard, which had its origins in the firm of Tod & McGregor, who began shipbuilding in Govan in 1838 and in 1844 moved across the river to Meadowside.

Across the mouth of the River Kelvin from Henderson's is A. & J. Inglis' Pointhouse shipyard, which began building there in 1862, having bought the yard from T. B. Seath who moved upriver to Rutherglen. Pointhouse was best known for its paddle steamers the last of which was the *Waverley*, built in 1947 and now the world's only seagoing paddle steamer. In 1899 the yard built the first *Waverley*, which was sunk at Dunkirk in 1940 during the Second World War.

Opposite the barrage balloon is Yorkhill Quay, the home of Anchor Line vessels, with Queen's Dock beyond.

To the left is Victoria Park, with Partick east of it. Ibrox is behind the Fairfield and Harland & Wolff ship-yards.

D. & W. Henderson's Meadowside yard seen here with a ship in its dry dock, in the late 1920s, continued shipbuilding until 1935 after which it carried out repair work until 1965. Apart from building Anchor Line vessels and Clyde steamers, the yard specialised in large yachts like *Britannia*, built in 1893 for the Prince of Wales, later Edward VII. The yard had the city's first dry dock, opened in 1858 by Tod & MacGregor. To the right is A. & J. Inglis' Pointhouse shipyard. In the foreground is Harland & Wolff's shipyard. The Govan ferry is crossing from Pointhouse.

Crown copyright RCAHMS Ref P309 009424

1. Prince's Dock
2. Govan Graving Docks
3. Harland & Wolff's Govan Shipyard
4. Fairfield Shipyard
5. Alexander Stephen's Linthouse Shipyard
6. Shieldhall Sewage Works
7. Charles Connell's Scotstoun Shipyard
8. North British Engine Works
9. Barclay Curle's Clydeholm Shipyard
10. Meadowside Quay and Granary
11. D. & W. Henderson's Meadowside Shipyard
12. A. & J. Inglis Pointhouse Shipyard
13. Yorkhill Quay and Basin
14. Queen's Dock

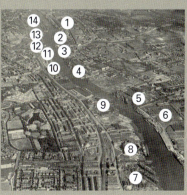

Index